POEMS

BY

GAY CLIFFORD

POEMS
BY
GAY CLIFFORD

.

Introduced by

GERMAINE GREER

HAMISH HAMILTON
LONDON

HAMISH HAMILTON LTD

Published by the Penguin Group
27 Wrights Lane, London W8 5TZ, England
Viking Penguin Inc., 40 West 23rd Street New York, New York 10010, USA
Pengin Books Australia Ltd, Ringwood, Victoria, Australia
Penguin Books Canada Ltd, 2801 John Street, Markham, Ontario,
Canada L3R 1B4
Penguin Books (NZ) Ltd, 182–190 Wairau Road, Auckland 10, New Zealand

Penguin Books Ltd, Registered Offices: Harmondsworth, Middlesex, England

First published 1990

Poems copyright © Gay Clifford, 1990
Introduction copyright © Germaine Greer, 1990

Typeset in Linotron Bembo at The Spartan Press Ltd,
Lymington, Hants
Printed in Great Britain by
Butler & Tanner, Frome

A CIP catalogue record for this book is available from the British Library

ISBN 0–241–129761

CONTENTS

·

vii

ACKNOWLEDGEMENTS

·

I would like to thank my parents, Pam and Freddie Clifford, and my friends Germaine Greer, Stoddard Martin, and Bill and Rosemary Righter for their love and help with this book.

INTRODUCTION

·

It was still winter that Sadie Hawkins Day in 1978, when Gay Clifford first showed me her poems. The day was shiny, carved by a sharp wind that kept the snow frozen and pushed the high white cloud away from the face of the sun. Gay had called me in New York as I was about to leave for London, to tell me with conspicuously brave understatement that, driving too fast on an icy road, she had written off her second-hand station wagon. I rejigged my travel so I could leave from Washington, but I had to wait several hours for a flight to Charlottesville and arrived tired, worried and late. Gay had prepared a pale lemony chicken dish that seemed the more wonderful to me because I had been on the lecture trail for three weeks, eating nothing but tuna salad sandwiches. The kitchen was not hers; we did not eat with her heavy old silver off the heavy white china plates she always got from Antinori in Rome, the table was not covered with one of her old white linen cloths, and we did not blot our mouths with her white damask napkins, but it was an elegant lunch. Gay's cooking and the wines she poured were always good.

'Couldn't Colonel Sanders have done the chicken?' I asked, ungraciously. I was cross that she had gone to so much trouble, and crosser that, by a dozen small grimaces that were not quite hidden, that I was meant to see but not to acknowledge, she was letting me know she was in pain.

When we had cleared the table and tidied up the kitchen (for Gay was the most orderly person, kept all her belongings in apple-pie order, labelled, folded, scented and camphored and clean) she produced a handful of typed papers and laid them before me. They were poems, among them 'Euripides' *Iphigenia in Aulis*' (p. 27), 'The departure' (p. 29), 'After the performance' (p. 31), 'Wolves; for my friend' (p. 35), 'A Garden Shut Up' (p. 43). I read them slowly, and read them again, saying over and over, 'Gay! Gay! You're a poet! A poet!' I simply couldn't get over it. Here, sitting a foot away, was my friend of more than ten years, and all the time she had been a poet and I hadn't known.

Delight began to bubble under the numbness of surprise. I had friends who had made of themselves career diplomats, senior politicians, premiated actors, musicians who had earned gold discs, but this was the double whammy, a poet! And she was my co-worker, my neighbour, my sister in affliction and delight, Gay Allis Rose Clifford. She was already distinguished as an academic, with a well-reviewed book to her credit and enthusiastic endorsements on her students' assessments; she was multi-lingual, well-dressed, entertaining, gave good parties dinner- and other, had a circle of loyal friends and a much wider circle of disloyal and envious acquaintances. If this had been all it would have been enough. That she should have the sumptuous impertinence to open her mouth and utter the higher truth, that she should be that unconscious conduit, a medium, a sacred creature, *vates*, made me quite giddy with joy. I was so chuffed that I went about for weeks telling old ladies at traffic lights, 'Guess what? One of my best friends is a poet!' 'Very nice for you too, dear,' they would say, with the placating smile and backward step that disarm lunatics.

Our friendship began inauspiciously. In the autumn of 1967, when news had come through of my appointment to the University of Warwick, a hard-drinking friend who had encountered Gay at Oxford said, 'Warwick! You'll have to endure the appalling Clifford.' On my first day there one of my senior colleagues, whose only claim to fame was that he had got the back of his head into a famous photo of Camus, asked me if I had met my sole female colleague yet. 'Very exotic,' he said. 'Long black hair, sort of oriental, silky. Large slanting brown eyes, bit Eurasian maybe. Hobnobs with the greats.'

The first time I spoke to Miss Clifford was in the secretary's office, where I was standing frozen with astonishment and pain at the sight of my first salary cheque.

'How do you manage?' I asked. She looked at me in cold surprise. 'I mean, how is one meant to live?'

'We manage,' she said crisply. I knew that she had a house and a car, but the cheque I held in my hand would not cover my food or my bus fares or even allow an occasional shilling for the gas meter in my miserable bedsit. Later I heard that she actually owned her little house in Kenilworth and gave select dinner parties there with French (rather than Bulgarian) wine. I soon discovered that I was not to expect any hospitality from my colleagues, and did my socializing with students. Miss Clifford and I met only in staff meetings where we were bound by a tacit solidarity, being the hardest worked members of the faculty not only because of the weight of routine chores and repetitive teaching dumped on junior female staff, but because of our extravagant accessibility to students. When the university registry was occupied in February 1968 we had no difficulty supporting the students' demands for democracy in education. There were political dossiers on both of us in the Vice-Chancellor's files. Gay was known to be a socialist; I was suspected of darker associations. I had been unable to get the support of Gay's friend E. P. Thompson for the anti-Vietnam war demonstrations in which as an Australian I was inextricably involved and the intolerance that members of the

3

left-wing reserve for each other divided us on other issues as well.

When in the summer of 1970 I first visited Gay and her lover, Michael, in the little Tuscan house called Pianelli, we still did not know each other very well. I had toiled up the steep and stony road on a frog-green moped, half the time running beside it because it would not handle the bends in the searing heat, and had surprised them both naked. Gay was, as usual, working, sweat dripping on to her books in the sun which had burned her as brown as a nut. The holiday rent was not cheap, and they were obliged to economize on food. Michael made unleavened flour and water biscuits, rather like outsized hosts, for tea, but the tea was Gunpowder.

A week or two later, looking out from my borrowed house on a neighbouring hillside, I saw a smoke-stain spreading up the sky and took off on my moped again, to see if help was needed to fight the fire. It was raging out of control; all hands were cutting and ploughing breaks. My best contribution was to act as liaison for we had no telephones or radios. First I went on up the hill to see if the fire was likely to burn down to the road, in which case Gay and Michael would have to be got out, for once it got to the road the fire would race up the valley to Pianelli in minutes. Gay's Renault stood ready packed by the door. That terrible night, when the firelight danced on the whitewashed walls as bright as day, and the roar of the flames advanced and retreated, and advanced again, and stands of Spanish broom many yards from the firefront whooshed into flame because of the great heat, Gay and I began to laugh at each other's jokes. The hill opposite the house burned from top to bottom, but the fire did not cross the road. In the morning we unpacked the car and ate figs for breakfast.

'Whew,' said Gay, 'in my sad opinion I was not like to behold a grasshopper, much less to pluck another fig.' Not knowing she was quoting Sir Thomas Browne, I had fain refer to baskets of figs and trails of aspic, which led to a good deal of nonsense about vile jellies of one sort or another, which the less pedantic reader would find tortuous and uninteresting.

Though I would venture to say that Gay understood me better than any other friend I have made since my teens, and we enjoyed each other's company in both riotous and tranquil modes, our friendship did not deepen into a settled intimacy. Gay had many friends I did not like and ambitions that I did not share. When she was in love, her lover got all her attention, whether he wanted it or not. Gay had no wish to confront my sarcasms about the candidates for her passionate attachment, not one of whom I liked or respected, the more because she had a completely unfounded belief that I was more successful with men than she. (The truth was that I expected a great deal less of men and was as a consequence less often disappointed.) I found myself having to compete for her attention, first with her man, then with her job, then with her wide circle of friends and acquaintances, and then with her continual money problems which, combined with her reluctance to accept even the most casual generosity, led to an endless series of misunderstandings.

The first and most serious misunderstanding was about Pianelli, for I bought the little house in the woods when I learned that it was not to be put up for rent any more, so that Gay could stay in it whenever she wanted, with or without me. On my first night in the house as owner, Gay and Michael moved out and slept elsewhere, so that I could gloat over my new acquisition alone. Later she was to tell people that I had taken the house from her. The responsibility for the misunderstanding is all mine, for I did not involve Gay in the decision to buy the house, did not consult her about its management, did not salve her self-esteem by demanding some sort of rent. I ran it as an autocracy, and though she did not object to my clearing the brambles away, raising the dry walls, and planting a garden, Gay clearly felt that the little house was no longer her territory and used it much less than I would have wanted.

One of the best times we had together was the ride home to England at the end of that summer. As Gay piloted her red Renault up the Autostrada del Sole, I tried to relieve the boredom by making eye contact with the drivers of any interesting cars that passed us. The most interesting was a dark brown Ferrari which flashed past, then slowed down to a crawl in front of us so that Gay had to pass it whereupon it zoomed past us and slowed down again. Gay became rather rattled as this procedure was repeated many times, and I realized that she was not in the habit of picking men up anywhere, let alone in the middle of a motorway. As we passed a sign advertising a restaurant a kilometre ahead the Ferrari driver began to signal that he was about to pull off the motorway.

'That's an invitation to lunch,' I observed. 'Do we accept it?'

Gay's only reply was to sweep past the restaurant exit where I could see the Ferrari pulled up. In a matter of seconds it was in front of us again, and the motorway courtship resumed. Gay was by now quite cross because she realized that she was running out of petrol. When we began to signal that we were pulling off at the next service station the Ferrari went on ahead.

'Do we accept lunch?' I asked, for the brown Ferrari was waiting at the foot of the steps up to the restaurant. By this time I was a bit uneasy myself, because I couldn't see how we were going to extricate ourselves from the situation. Gay walked grimly towards the restaurant. The driver of the Ferrari, choosing his moment, leapt out of his beautiful car and walked hopefully towards us. He was short, squat, pot-bellied and bald. Gay and I looked at each other and burst out laughing. '*Non auriga piger*. God knows what we expected,' said Gay helplessly. 'Mazeppa? The Aga Khan?' We did not let him buy our lunch.

Three hundred yards inside the Mont Blanc tunnel we had a flat tyre. Gay changed it in three minutes, while I stood directing traffic away from our exposed rear end. The tunnel tow-truck came roaring up. 'Why didn't you use the emergency phone?' the man asked angrily. 'It's illegal to change tyres in the tunnel.'

'Oh dear. Please forgive us, we didn't know,' lied Gay contritely, turning away his wrath with a 500-watt smile, as she threw the damaged tyre into the boot. As we pulled away I could see through the soupy tunnel smog the breakdown man still standing nonplussed in front of his truck wondering how such a pretty lady managed to change a tyre rather more quickly than he could.

That night we stayed in the Hotel du Beau Rivage in Geneva. As Gay, who had done all the driving, soaked away the aches in a deep marble bath, I plied her with chilled Dom Perignon, 'the true, the *un*blushing Hippocrene'. When we came down the great dining room was empty but for a dozen waiters who flocked around our table, competing for the pleasure of serving *Lapin à la moutarde* to two good-looking ladies already a-twinkle with good champagne.

The next day at the frontier the Swiss customs men took away what Gay called my pisspot because they thought it smelt peculiar and presented it to a dog. We got it back twenty minutes later soaking wet and full of teeth marks. 'All things considered,' said Gay as I dropped the smelly thing back in my bag, 'I think I prefer patchouli to tongue of dog.' We are both cat-women.

Gay and I played word games all the way to Calais, not all of them erudite; Gay is responsible for my enduring habit of referring to the source of all our woes as 'Westmonster' and the railways as 'Brutish Rail'. Our ingenuity was eclipsed by a placard in the middle of the road that read: 'Attention. Danger. Nids de Poule!' This set us off on a hard-fought game of 'hens in literature' which was crowned by the sight of an illuminated sign for a motel for wine buyers calling itself a 'Henotel'. The 'Henotel' is still there and every time I pass by I remember how our ribs ached that night. That night belongs to the distant past that is all that Gay can remember now, and I can still make her laugh by talking about the strangeness of Normandy where the nests of dangerous hens are found on the crown of the road.

One December, I won the competition for Gay's company at Christmas. We set off in a rust-riddled Fiat 2600, embellished with copious chromium trim and fins fore and aft, the property of my secretary. The car had failed its MOT and on a whim I decided to take it back to Italy to see if reconstruction of its crumbling nether parts was feasible. Gay knew that there was little likelihood of the car's getting us to our destination for it was falling to pieces even as we looked at it; nevertheless she agreed to come. We equipped ourselves with fur coats, partly because the Tuscan hills can be bitterly cold in winter, but mostly because we wanted to look flash enough to get the best out of the people we might have need of on the way. When I started the enormous engine it uttered a throbbing roar like a small plane and we taxied rather than drove off towards Dover.

Minutes later there was a muted crash, followed by a teeth-jarring series of scrapes and crunches. I peered under our tail section, but all I could see was a sort of ribbon of rusty metal trailing on the ground. I rolled it up so that it hung clear and we continued on our booming progress. It was pitch dark when we taxied out of Calais, and a good deal darker when for arcane reasons connected with the elderly wiring the lights in the Fiat's instrument panel went out. We had to drive with the windows open in order to make hand signals, which rendered conditions undeniably bleak even before we realized that the heating wasn't working either. We pulled our fur collars up snug around our freezing faces, unscrewed the cap on our duty-free Laphroaig and generally emulated the sledded Polacks on the ice.

Next morning, when we had got as far as Lyons there came a very loud crash, followed by an earsplitting grating, as if the car's behind had fallen off. I free-wheeled off the carriageway of the urban autoroute into a *chantier* marked off by oil drums and got out to inspect the damage. A sort of fat steel cushion was lying on the ground between the rear wheels. Flics were converging on us from every direction. Gay swung her legs out of the car in a slightly more exhibitionist fashion than usual and prepared a smile of the utmost delight and confidence with which to greet them. I was trying not to think about the danger of a hideous conflagration and concentrate on my lady-of-fashion-mystified-by-motors act. The gendarmes fell for the whole routine; as we stood chatting about 'la belle France' and our passionate attachment to the Midi, Provence, *Cimetière marin* and all that, one of them ran, actually ran to get a mechanic and both of them ran back with a hydraulic jack. The car's finny rump was hoisted up, the mechanic crawled underneath and within minutes had lashed the petrol tank back on with his tow-rope which he tied in a floppy bow on the roof. It was decided that we had to take the car to the workshop but hélas the next exit was some kilometres down the road and we would have to make our way back through city streets . . . It was all *vachement dangereux, vous comprenez*. It was by now lunchtime and all the bons Lyonnais were on their way home for lunch. Two of the gendarmes walked back the way we had come to the exit we had just passed and, in one of the most foolhardy stunts I have ever seen, raised their left hands so that amid the most appalling screaming of brakes and blasting of horns, the great river of cars was brought to a halt. Then with their right hands they directed the cars off the motorway and into the side streets. The drivers howled and gesticulated; the gendarmes held their ground.

I let the clutch in, wheeled the great car around and taxied up the motorway in the wrong direction, while Gay waved and blew kisses to the gendarmes who stood to attention.

They brought up their hands to their képis and gravely saluted as the great car nosed along at a monarch's pace, the loops of its hairy bow drooping on each side like elephant's ears.

Needless to say the Lyonnais mechanic's boss had no intention of involving himself in the thankless task of trying to reattach our petrol tank to the Fiat's rotten chassis, although he made us wait until he had finished his lunch to tell us so. He was made of sterner stuff than the flics and none of our multilingual charms worked on him. When he shrugged and walked away for the tenth time, I gave up. 'Let's go,' said Gay, 'I should be loath to lay out money on a rope.' We boomed off through the streets of Lyons back to the motorway.

'I don't think we'll get far,' I said dubiously. Every hundred kilometres or so I had to check that the exhaust pipe wasn't burning through the rope. We prepared for battle with those guardians of public safety who would have objected to our hazardous progress, but none eventuated. In the wee hours we got to the Italian border but so touched were the border police at our exclamations of innocent delight at being at last in Italy that they failed to notice our elephant ears. We could only half fill the petrol tank, and had no petrol gauge, so twice we panted to a dead stop. Twice Gay grabbed the red can, sprinted across the carriageway, and stuck her thumb out. Each time she was back in ten minutes. We were a hell of a team. After three days without sleep, when we and the Fiat were at last at Pianelli, Gay and I were still laughing at each other's jokes.

When I woke up in the little house at Pianelli that Christmas morning there was a proper red stocking hanging at the foot of my bed. It was stuffed with all kinds of thoughtful little things, all exactly calculated to appeal to my rather unpredictable tastes and obsessions. Gay had amassed them over weeks and weeks and brought them ready wrapped in her suitcase from England. Usually I open presents in a state of anguish brought on by having to pretend to want the things that other people want to give me. This time as I unwrapped each little package and found six real tortoise-shell buttons, a marzipan cat, a necklace of Venetian glass daisies, a phial of bergamot oil, a nutmeg-holder, a Roman lachrymatory, a tuning-fork, and, in the toe, cassettes of Karl Böhm's recording of *The Magic Flute* I felt, besides unalloyed and unfeigned pleasure, a slight shake at the heart as I wondered if I understood anyone as well as Gay understood me.

It was not an easy matter to build on that understanding. Though Gay bought the basement flat of my house in North Kensington, she mostly let it and seldom stayed there. When she was there she often chose to be inaccessible. When I was in hospital having an operation Gay borrowed the house to stay in with the man she eventually married; I came home, unable to lift anything heavier than a teapot and expecting to see them, but they had moved on. I sat at the foot of the stairs with my suitcase for an hour or two, and then locked the house up and checked into a hotel. Gay never so much as enquired how I did. She was in love with a mere mortal who had to be protected from me if she was going to see it through.

She was living with him in Virginia when she showed me the poems. He drove me to Washington airport, complaining all the way that Gay was desperate to be married. 'Hell,' he said, 'I've been married all my life. The divorce isn't final from my second wife yet and Gay wants me to get married again. She makes these terrible scenes, hitting and screaming. She won't leave me alone about it. Jesus. She wants to be married in Westminster Abbey with me in dress blues.'

I was stupid enough to be astonished. Though she espoused fashionable feminism I should have known that Gay had never been against marriage. The man she wanted was an ex-marine whom she described 'as the strawberry blond patriarch' because he had four children by two wives. He was tall, handsome and clever, a published writer and career academic, and he had a distinguished military record. I thought him a second-rater; I knew what Washington hostesses said of him and I was convinced that a man who had made two women unhappy enough to divorce him would not bring happiness to a third.

Eventually I said, 'Gay wants her babies. It's time for her to have her babies. If you don't want to be part of it, you should back out now. Don't waste her time.' He protested that he had never had such brilliant sex, and couldn't give it up. I reflected bitterly on the unfortunate consequences of trying to do everything perfectly. That night he told Gay that I had warned him that she was desperate for marriage and children. From then until the wedding Gay stayed away from me and from Pianelli.

When I got back to England I wrote to Gay, 'Kingsley Amis agrees that it is the most uncommonly unsettling and gratifying thing to find that a loved one is inflated with the divine gas. I feel the oddest and most disreputable mass of feelings, the most unwelcome being astonishment and a sort of fright, as if you had suddenly taken off from a balcony and were flapping around the house in defiance of gravity, but worst of all a sort of rage that you might suddenly take to marriage and write your poems on a corner of the kitchen table while the bread is proving . . .' The letter was not entirely disingenuous. The name was dropped on purpose. I wanted her to tell me the truth about her feelings, but she never did.

Even more disreputable than astonishment and fright were the feelings I did not tell Gay about. The earliest dated poem was three months old when I read it; it was as if she had given birth to a child and told me three months afterwards. Other people, perhaps many other people, had seen Gay's poems before I knew that they existed. I could not bring myself to ask why she had waited so long to share

12

this immense discovery of herself as a poet with me. The question was too near the knuckle. I was afraid she was worried that by a reductive judgment or, worse, by ridicule I would bruise her talent before it had hardened by exposure, and bring her best efforts to nothing. I knew that one of Gay's avatars loved me, another admired, another feared, yet another envied, and one hated me as one competitor in a tough race has to hate another. My hand shook as I read the poems because I felt that distrust had gained the mastery, but I said nothing of this. In her poem about this occasion, Gay says that I said, 'Consider delusion, but jump.' And that she said, 'Now I have my voice.' In that poem, 'Finalities' (p. 39), her voice is blurred, distorted by my mediation. I have not always been good for her.

If Gay feared my jaundiced editorial eye, she feared her own critical self no less. My deepest anxiety for Gay Clifford, poet, was that the conflict between her analytic, eclectic, professional academic self and the almost new-born self I had only just encountered would tear her to pieces. I knew most of Gay's voices, and the first I had ever heard that was totally authentic was the voice that could be heard throughout 'The departure' (p. 29). It is a poem written in the full awareness of what English poetry is and has been for a thousand years, but it makes no display of learning; there is no glitter of cleverness, no dramatic flourish, nothing but poise, reflectiveness, and rhythm, 'the movement of all the songs she knew'. In the resolution of that poem I saw my friend whole and clear, with all her masks dropped away. And I was jealous that the sight was there for all those with eyes to see. I feared too that the magic concatenation of circumstances, that allowed the synthesis of all that my friend was and could be, would unlink and fall once more into disharmony, leaving her more bereft than she had ever been before. I could not have been more afraid for her if I had seen her crossing Cheddar Gorge on a tightrope.

For the life of me I could not understand what the key was

that in her thirty-fifth year had turned in synchrony all the tumblers of Gay's intricate personality and opened the way for her true self. I wrote to her, 'If Virginia unleashes the poetry, Virginia deserves you as we do not, for we seem to have locked it up in you. I feel tired and nervous when it occurs to me that I have lost a friend, and one so long in the making.' The discovery that Gay is a poet was made on the brink of our longest estrangement. Under the heading 'Virginia' I included the man Gay was in love with. For all I knew he was one of the empowering circumstances that had enabled Gay to speak with her own poetic voice. I fully expected that she would give up her academic post in England and stay in Virginia with him. I even hoped that he would support her while she wrote, for I had not the least doubt that the greatest enemy that her poetry faced was that vague complex we call 'academe'.

Gay, like all young, single, female academics, worked too hard. The number of hours she had to teach in England was very much higher than would have been expected on any American campus, and perhaps the poetry had emerged because she actually had some time free from preparing lectures and seminars, correcting essays and dissertations, attending endless faculty meetings and teaching and counselling students. Gay did not simply carry out her allotted tasks. She did not merely do what was expected of her and so miserably paid; she was over-prepared for her teaching, over-scrupulous in her marking, utterly involved with her students' problems. Her social life was run with the same intensity and perfectionism. Even when she took a night off and went to the cinema, she chose a testing film and prepared to understand it and to memorize every sequence. Like a marathon runner she was constantly competing with herself, pushing herself beyond her limits, and long before that frosty day in Virginia the finite part of her, her body, had begun to exact its revenge.

In 1974 Routledge and Kegan Paul published what Gay once called in a letter to me her 'paltry, little book', *Transformations of Allegory*. By no means paltry, it is a sinuous and graceful exposition of multi-layered utterance, as well-read and thorough as one would expect of the Gay Clifford who won a first at Oxford in 1964. It was *Transformations of Allegory* as much as anything that screened from me the possibility that Gay would be prompted to invent her own visions and figure forth her own truth. It hardly seemed necessary after all; Gay had such a vocabulary of other people's incantations that she could not open her mouth but straight there flew a trope, either a direct quotation or some phrase or motif adapted to her purpose. Both of us were so imbued with English poetry that we sometimes wondered whether we did not experience our own lives in other people's words.

'Euripides' *Iphigenia in Aulis*', which was written on the same day as 'The departure', is a less personal poem, and more typical of Gay Clifford's imaginative method. It was natural to her to explore all the variations on the theme of a given text, and she was struck by a number of symmetrical and contradictory aspects of the myth of Iphigenia. In Euripides' version, Artemis demanded the sacrifice of the female child and Artemis rescued her, leaving a deer in her place; Euripides was himself killed by hunting dogs in the same way as Actaeon who was turned into a deer for spying on the virgin goddess Artemis and her nymphs as they bathed. The state poet who justifies the institutionalized predation that is war becomes himself a female figure, a victim; the tissue of the poem is twisted tight by Gay Clifford's keen awareness of what it is to be a female interpreter of male supremacist culture. The bitterness is most effective where it is under complete and cool control as it is in this, Gay Clifford's first surviving poem.

'Against Yeats' (p. 65), written a year later, is another wry attack on the tradition, called forth this time by Yeats's

'Leda and the Swan'. We were all soaked in Yeats, who seemed to us a far better poet than Eliot, but there was no denying his racism, sexism and downright fascism. We resented 'A Prayer for my Daughter' just as we resented the absurd phallocentricity of the Yeatsian view of history. The male supremacist threat became pure humbug when it was our moth-eaten male colleagues who expounded it, 'vague fingers pushing across a page' following the description of Leda's 'terrified vague fingers'. The poet, like a distracted student, reacts to the laboured identification of the rape of Leda as the cause of Helen's vengeful adultery and the Trojan War, by imagining the swan as a figure of the Holy Ghost and coming up with the cunt-struck, tarred and feathered figure of Papageno, leading her to a last and monstrous pun, that of the swan's 'unpaid bill'.

Gay was gratified and not in the least surprised when she received rejection letters that twittered on about 'raw energy', a 'little too wild for our list'. Wildness was what she was striving for, not barbarism or savagery, for both were beyond her, but the wildness of spontaneously occurring things, of elusive self-regulating creatures, be they cowslips or swallows. In the struggle to escape the bonds of her other-directed, examination-passing, dead-line-meeting superego, Gay Clifford did sometimes descend to cant and rant. In her least successful poems there is a palpable attempt to whip up emotion, a pinching and wringing of her own flesh. In the selection of Gay Clifford's work assembled in this book the editors have tried to exclude what seemed to us shallow and self-dramatizing. Many otherwise fine poems are disfigured by spasms of posturing and bombast, false notes which would have been expunged by the poet upon reworking, but as Gay's condition deteriorated she became progressively less capable of reworking and less inclined to it. Some of her most imperfect poems are also the most interesting, and we make no apology for including them. We know only 152 poems, of which we have included eighty-nine; Gay was prodigal with her occasional verse, and there will be more poems in the possession of others of her friends.

I was probably wrong in feeling that Gay had gone through a period of gestation and told me nothing about it. The poetry erupted with astonishing suddenness. In the last week of January, 1978, Gay wrote five poems; the next week two more. These early poems were several times reworked and revised. It was a risky business, for Gay knew only too well that in reworking she might crush the life out of her poetry. Her insecurity, the insecurity of every creative person for whom each utterance is a raid on the unknown, could hardly resist the onslaught of her trained faculty of interpretation and evaluation. Her poems could not be anything other than eclectic; this in itself would not be a disadvantage. Pound and Eliot are preposterously eclectic. All poetry is constructed out of fragments of the past; our very language is a living fossil record, but if these bones are to sing they must first be allowed to live. Gay struggled to imbue the reminiscences of all she knew and all she was with new life.

If any single theory of poetics lay behind Gay Clifford's method it was almost certainly that of William Empson, whom she greatly admired; her poetry is deliberately allusive and ambiguous, turning key concepts and archetypal images over and over, so that new insights flash from them. In 'Burnt we do burne' a motif from *The Faerie Queene* provides the staple for a fabric that interweaves non-literary experience, both historical and personal. The shield of Atin, *agent provocateur* for his lord, Pyrochles, shows

> A flaming fire in midst of bloudy field,
> And round about the wreath this word was writ,
> *Burnt I do burne.*

The poet uses the reminiscence of Sir Guyon and his fight with extremism of all kinds in the exercise of the sovereign virtue of temperance as a point from which to contemplate the holocausts of recent history. Themselves burnt by the murderous violence of Nazis, the British invented the firestorms of Dresden and Hamburg. When Gay and I lived in the same house in North Kensington we were obliged to give assistance to the victims of street violence, West Indians, old ladies, drunken tinkers and policemen, all burnt and burning with outrage and pain. A *graffito* on the wall at the end of the street screamed, 'This too will burn', another, 'Even the sky will burn'. The wildfires that we had watched raging around Pianelli were laid by a mad old man who had watched his valley die first by war, then by *miseria*, and then the lingering, dishonourable death by tourism. (Now they daren't let him out of prison, for he will burn the hills again. Gay would have made much of that.) Gay Clifford knew too that the soul is the fire in the clay, and that to recoil from the burning hills and seek the quiet plain is to stifle the Promethean urge that brings about all change. All these elements are present in 'Burnt we do burne', together with Gay Clifford's dissatisfaction with her scruples, for as intellectuals we radicals dare not fight fire with fire. The hammer and the sickle remain alike unused. The Spenser chime controls and shapes the feeling, just as Gay Clifford's patrician culture was the matrix for her socialist politics. Her socialism was a matter of conviction, but she yearned for ceremony and elegance. The contradiction (which is by no means logically necessary) caused her great pain.

Not only was Gay Clifford trained into a critical habit of mind, she was also deeply attached to the themes and conventions of the literature, and in particular the medieval literature, she had spent her life studying. Terzains and quatrains, villanelles and canzonets, repetitive refrains rang through her head. Highly wrought figures of alliteration and metonymy, prosopopaeiae and skipping and clipping rhythms were as natural to her as riffs to a drummer. At first she repressed these echoes and wrote principally in free verse. Now and then she tried to spin such formal structures into poetry but the energy drained from the ideas as she worked them. Disheartened she let her still-born rhymes lie, disfigured with extra feet and missing syntactic elements, eclipsed by their remembered refrains, waiting perhaps for a day when she would know how to rework them. Some of these deformed beauties we have included (see for example, 'She was linden, . . .', p. 114, 'Self portrait', p. 117, 'You knew it then . . .', p. 120, 'Once I came from silence and lies . . .', p. 128). To those of us who care about Gay they are moving; to those who care about poetry they are more moving still.

The truest history is the most feigning; Gay Clifford has always had a horror of bald plain-speaking which she regarded as verbal brutality, crushing nuance, closing off all escape, extorting submission, driving benign hypocrisy and courtesy out of reach. She resented the self-plunder, the immodesty and exposure that are demanded of poets in our time, and again and again used the metaphor of being eaten up (see for example 'Reader', p. 56). Among the ancient conventions that she loved and longed to shelter behind was that of exaggerating the humility of the poet, and thus allowing his arrogance to flourish. Many of her poems are conscious celebrations, public gifts from the extravagant *fabbro* to an unwitting (and undeserving) patron, who might well cringe. She has a trick of panegyric which is easily confused with gushing, especially as underneath there has always been a shifting ground of self-doubt and insecurity about her friends, their essential nature and their commitment to her. Like all such doubt it is thoroughly justified, but Gay insisted on ennobling the life she shared with her friends by celebrating them. Her words were after all more real and durable than their nature. She used epithets the way the Greeks used them, to glorify and thereby create glory, so that her friends would be magnified, become larger than life, for being praised creates praise-worthiness.

'Finalities' is disfigured by such compliment, which may easily degenerate to bombast. I did not see the poem until long after it was written, and even then did not grasp that it was meant to be my *congedo*. For many years I was struck by the flattery and the glamorizing – my eyes are not turquoise and the bracelet was not lapis – and did not notice that the flattery was in the past tense. I had been dismissed, more, it would seem from the poem's rhetoric, in sorrow than in anger. I learned of the stormy progress of Gay's courtship and marriage at a distant remove. She told me nothing; she even passed within yards of Pianelli without coming up to hug the cats or see the garden. People who knew us to be friends telephoned me to complain of Gay's bizarre and inconsiderate behaviour, and to ask an explanation of me who could least supply it. I hoped that Gay, who had always been the perfect hostess and the perfect guest (never forgot her bread-and-butter letter) as well as the most punctilious and reliable of academics, was breaking out and not breaking down. She was actually doing both. One of the wards of the key that opened the door to her poetic voice was Gay's illness, the same illness that was to silence that voice for ever. In her beginning was her end.

My wish that Gay Clifford would have time to collect herself and write, undepleted by the omnivorous demands she made on herself as a teacher, was not granted. At the end of the summer of '78 she returned to England. Her academic career was approaching its apogee; the years of hard work in the provinces were about to be rewarded by an appointment to University College, London. There was not the slightest possibility that Gay would cleave to her lover and her poetry and let her profession go hang; she had given it too much and it was the one aspect of her life that had never failed her. The stress of the three-way conflict

between love, duty and poetry produced some extraordinary work.

Gay knew that she had to transcend an academic's height-
ened consciousness of failure if she was to write poetry at all.
She did not have the trumpeting ego that protects the artist
from vertigo, and she did not have the necessary ego-support
system because she was a woman, a heterosexual woman
living in the house of her enemy. There is no point in
identifying the male antagonist in Gay's poetic universe as
any specific person, least of all her husband, who never
grasped the enormity of Gay's fate. The 'he' of Gay's poetry
is most profitably construed as the generic male, who abused
her more by his little-boy indifference to anything but his
own convenience and trivial pleasure than by deliberate
cruelty or hostility. More insidious was the pressure that Gay
applied to herself, her need to be the ultimate, the perfect, the
unforgettable lover. Spontaneity was the thing she found
hardest; her poetry demanded it. She could not supply
spontaneity until her narcissistic super-ego had been put out
of action, so she sabotaged it herself.

Gay's struggle and its destructive consequences are prefig-
ured in 'Invocation' by Kathleen Raine:

> There is a poem on the way . . .
> it hovers, a spirit
> that I would make incarnate.
> Let my body sweat
> let snakes torment my breast
> my eyes be blind, ears deaf, hands distraught
> mouth parched, uterus cut out,
> belly slashed, back lashed,
> tongue slivered into thongs of leather
> rain stones inserted in my breasts,
> head severed,
>
> if only the lips may speak
> if only the god will come.

If I had understood what was going on, I should indeed have fought to save Gay, for I loved her better than her poetry. I went to her wedding reception as the stone guest, a death's head at the feast; I visited her in hospital after an operation to alleviate the worst effects of Crohn's Disease, but most of the time I was away in Oklahoma, in India or absorbed in my own work. By the time she agreed to come to Pianelli with me in 1982 it was too late.

We drove through extraordinary torrents of rain, so that we seemed to be proceeding under water. Gay was uncomplaining, but withdrawn and shrunken. She was submitting to my will in that she drank nothing but a glass or two of wine at meals, but the result was far from heartening. Then one day she seemed to come to life; colour came back into her cheeks and she began to joke again. She scribbled a poem and left it on my desk, doodling on the paper as she made a series of uproarious and expensive phone calls. We went to friends for dinner and they looked on silent while Gay chattered hectically, repeating herself many times. Then she collapsed and we took her home. It was many weeks before I discovered that a bottle of aquavit that I had brought back from some trip and forgotten had been unearthed and drunk. I was too late; Gay had no spirit but what came from pills and the bottle, and no choice but to pursue what she saw as her destiny. She was a maenad about her own sparagmos. I could only watch and wait for the catastrophe, knowing that although she was racked with pain and shaking herself to pieces with synthetic energy, she was nearer to happiness than she had ever been, singing on her bed of nails high and aloof.

From the beginning of her short poetic career Gay was very interested in achieving recognition. 'The departure' was the first of seven poems to be published in various issues of *Encounter*, then 'Conjunction' (p. 71), 'Things moved are, usually, better' (p. 69), 'Against Yeats' (p. 65), 'Virginia; the Old Dominion', Summer 1981 (p. 86), 'Cats and all' (p. 99) and 'Demise of a middle class' (p. 166). *London Review of Books* published 'Confession' (p. 89) in 1981, *Poetry Review* June, 1983 published 'I will consider my cat Thisbe' (p. 100). *Over Our Dead Bodies: Women Against the Bomb* edited by Dorothy Thompson (Virago, 1983) included three poems by Gay Clifford, 'The cellars of Sidon' (p. 155), 'Something for Victor Jarra: vox populi' (p. 113) and 'Secret heroine from Joseph Conrad' (p. 97). 'Notes on the characters of men' (p. 102) appeared in *Avantgarde*, Summer 1981. 'Going to sleep with your rings on' (p. 60) won the Greenwich Festival First Prize in 1979, and was published in *Ambit*, as was 'The horseman remembers', No. 87 (p. 45). Gay was one of the editors of *Writing Women*, in which 'Euripides' *Iphigenia in Aulis*' appeared, Vol. I, No. 2. 'For Douglas' appeared in issue 8 of *Daimon*, the magazine of the Atlantic Poetry Collective and 'A Garden Shut Up' (p. 43) and 'Ballad for a Fair Lady' (p. 58) in *Daimon* 12. 'Mrs Pinkerton, Widow of Admiral Pinkerton, U.S.N.' (p. 67) was published in the anthology produced by the Lancashire Literary Festival 1980, *Women their World*; 'Necessary snobs' appeared in *Status UK* for Spring, 1987.

Gay Clifford's poetry is not a series of specimens to be of use in illustrating her case history. The editors make no apology for withholding details of names, dates and places, whether they refer to the men Gay loved, the houses she lived in, the hospitals she suffered in, the doctors who treated her, or the bacilli that feasted on her ravaged body. We have included only the notes she supplied herself when preparing her poems for publication in 1984. Gay Clifford's poetic career ended on Christmas Eve, 1984, when a cerebral haemorrhage devastated her brain. She is not dead or likely to die. Though there are some who might say it would be better if she were dead, they would be wrong. There is a strange mercy in the fact that Gay who so seldom relaxed and savoured the present is now forced to live only in the present, and she imposes the same necessity on those around her. After a friendship full of misunderstanding, now that so much less is said and written between us we are beginning to get each other right.

The poems are not exhibits at an inquest, but living documents of a struggle, which may illuminate the struggles of others who attempt to adapt the language of the ruling class to express their authenticity. Perhaps women who are in love with poetry are already lost; perhaps they can only parrot their masters' language or stridently abuse it to declaim against itself. We do not know and cannot imagine what the outcome of the struggle for the democratization of the means of expression will be. We live in an era when thousands of people write verse, and nobody reads it. We have not had a bestseller in verse since *Childe Harold*. Today's hordes of DIY poets do not bother to read poems by other people because they so enjoy penning their own.

Gay Clifford knew only too well how bitter is the fate of women trying to obey the peremptory demands of their own creativity within the limits imposed by our culture. She knew how Elizabeth Browning malingered, how Christina Rossetti tormented herself, how Tsvetayeva and Plath died, but she feared more than self-destruction the possibility that she would fall short and write in a minor, sentimental, archaizing, feminine rather than female way. She was aiming for the top of the glass mountain in the full knowledge of the terrible consequences if she fell. Gay Clifford the well-read, the thorough, the hard-working, the reliable, the punctilious, tore herself to pieces trying to say something truer than fact. Her monument was less than half-hewn when she was forced to abandon it, but it is more picturesque, more moving, grander, more sublime perhaps for that.

THE POEMS

Euripides' Iphigenia in Aulis

Artemis demanded the sacrifice:
Your daughter, or the fleet will stay,
There will be no wind
and Troy and the rape unpunished.
Even punitive Gods at times tire of attrition.
Perhaps this demand was meant to be outrageous
that even a vaunting King would refuse
and some peace begin.
But men's war had to prevail,
Iphigenia went to the knife and the altar,
so Artemis snatched her up and left a deer.

Artemis, were you inconsistent?
it was your own poet, Euripides,
he who told your demands, the father's need for
      victory,
and your intervention,
Who died in Macedonia, killed by hunting dogs –
you must have remembered Actaeon,
who hunting, saw your women naked,
and just to have seen them was itself ambition.
Actaeon sprouted horns, was transformed to soft-
      ness,
flesh to be sacrificed for appetite,
was eaten by dogs.

Perhaps some kinds of truth are too true to be
      spoken,
to state some kinds of knowledge invokes penalty.

To say that a woman's body must be slit
if the war is to go on,
and to say that women know it
(Meek Iphigenia, glossing self-abnegation
as patriotism, as selfless furtherance
of further slitting, more assertion of self by killing)
Is to risk for yourself
being the victim, being the patient,
like she you lament as the usual barter of war.

The hunt, the pursuit, the sacrifice,
shallow metaphors for eating up others.
Construct your plays on such pretences
and the horns sprout, your ambition simply equips
    you
to learn in your flesh what seemed theatrical form.

Entirely consistent, this ironic reminder
That if you make play of familiar cannibalism
You'll learn what it is to be torn,
Meet that pack of dogs, see their teeth,
Find your complicit sprouting
Is meat to the eating.
Euripides, the author of the *Bacchae*,
Presumably knew that metaphors of desire
Consume their progenitors, not their subjects,
Chronicled the consuming greed
For Iphigenia and success of war,
And became himself Iphigenia to the dogs.

25 i 78
21 ix 78

The departure

She had always dreaded his going, knew
That his absence would be the most complete failure,
And planned against it.

Yet when he went, her head sang, the music grew
    fresh;
There was nothing but pleasure, and exposure was
    only freedom.
Without me you are a shadow: but in the departure
He proved her solid. The deprival was only song.

Things became themselves and the space and silence
Hung with all she had lost. A rain of pleasure
Fell on the emptiness and made it a singing void.
Querulous need of consorting became the half-
    notes
Of solitude and in the space sang and echoed
All the voices she had heard: voices of the past
(Which he had, with peremptory tone,
Determined were not to be heard)
They were as tunes to her own self.
Her feet moved without the weight of present
    possession
And danced in lightness of remembered self.

He came again and demanded repossession,
And suddenly she could not remember
Why he should call the tune.

The piper was hers, she played the notes of silence
And absence echoed what she most desired.

He thought that going was a move of power.
His absence was the movement of all the songs she
    knew.

25 i 78

After the performance

You leave something in the theatre,
After a performance:
You must plead with the manager,
Cajole the doorman, bribe the departing staff.
Then, you get to the auditorium,
Hurrying back to your place,
Making sure the seat, its number now inverted,
Was really yours.

There are chocolate papers, suggesting expense
Appropriate to celebratory occasions;
The ruffled pile of carpet intended to meet
The needs of those who claim
That a place designed for public histrionics
Have the trodden luxury of the private theatre,
The close-piled living-room where antagonists
Heap insults without respect for prosody.

You search, you crawl, and the impatience of others
Reminds you of the insignificance of loss.
What you have left was sign of your own folly,
A mere detail. You need to reclaim it
That not only it may be yours, but that the evening
Can be yours again, as you bear home
The props with which you came to meet
The performance of passions trivial
Besides those your own play pre-enacted.

You become guilty, you are imposing on the
    manager.
You cannot find what you left.
To retrieve your losses, imaginary or real,
Seems presumption. Autobiography demands
Constant retrieval, yet to ask that
You find again what you had in the theatre
Is to claim for memory too much.
Your history has its props, but once
They become dependent on the time of others,
And their control of space, you are embarrassed
Before those who feel the acts are over.

Leavings of our past, detritus of the performance,
Are made to seem stale. There is no repossession.
You should have been paying more attention at the
    time.
Why did you applaud?
Not keep your hands on your lap?
Why did you not hold on to what was yours?

I thought the play was what I lived, what I knew,
Who I played. And present illusion
Suggested loosening hold on what I had.
Crass delusion, you had it as you acted.
How should you now hope to repossess it?

25 i 78

Symptoms of fear

The poet said:
'Courage means running'.
He was right, perhaps
Saving the courage in yourself
Sometimes needs running from fear of others.

Besides, fear's contagious.
The spores fall on the skin, it blisters
and bubbles and runs
and every orifice, irrational receptive
sucks in sticky poison.
Old lesions flower desperately,
The eyes run and film, seeing
only objects to keep fear alive.
The nose rots down two holes
only to snuff up your own folly.
Organs of generation hum
breeding fearful plague to others.

So who'd not run to quarantine
The subtle organs, cornea, cortex,
Cervix, wit and heart where safety
Allows healthy brave existence?

She'll not run who thinks
how bodies live on rot:
Skin a swarm of bacteria
devouring matter else would kill us,

Blood alive with phagocytes' consumption,
their canny greed for the infecting microbes;
And the meticulous ecology of bowels
where the bacillus is a kind utility
(Get sunstroke and the gut is too well purged:
you must crush ampoules of infection,
eat them so you again can eat).

Perhaps infection is the premiss, fear a decay
that eats up clotted courage,
the old, stiff, brave accretions.
To be ourselves alive perhaps
we need to fear, to feel
that vivid invasion of others
things not ourselves, and being not our own.
Fear sits in the skirts of the horseman
Fleeing his own self.
If I turn and ride to the heart of my own fear
To the city of plague I find
Infection benign, and courage
a fearful health, a blank white sepulchre.
Fear is symptom of life, symbiosis,
all infection matter for growth.
As I breathe in fear I feel decay
And live to others' breeding fear and life.

5 ii 78

Wolves; for my friend

The circus troupe played at the Alhambra Theatre.
Rain had flooded the site at the edge of town
where dark woods met the discipline of concrete;
lightning had ripped open the tent
leaving viscera of chairs and benches and sawdust;
wind had flattened the booths to Hiroshima
  shadows
against the neat paint of desirable residences.
The town clerk was a socialist who took pains
for gypsies and players and freaks needing a place
to earn tenuous bread by the whim of wage-earners;
he arranged the lease of the theatre.

The audience was motley, sweaty
Friday-night families in the gods
hanging over the stalled bourgeois
risking slumming in safe gentility.
The acts were odd. A stage is more open than the
  ring
where the hydra surrounds the juggling
with savagery. One act alone, the wolf and his man,
seemed neither silly nor flat.
The tamer had gold trunks, black boots and a
  bullwhip,
and the wolf ran under the lash seriously
meaning rage. The bared teeth could really rip,

35

and those haunches vault footlights
and satined thighs and make bloodily for the forest.
Sweat poured down the waxed moustache and
    smile
became rictus belied by the nerves at the whip:
this beast could kill us they murmured.
Then lights up, a tearing of fastenings
from throat to groin, and a boy stepped from the
    skin.
The trainer looked cowed and hairy, and sighs of
    relief
froze in the glacial menace of a young man's smile.
Golden, polite, his smile glittered,
and his hair fell softly down as he bowed.
He was impeccable, he should have reassured
but dread curdled the smoke and the sighs
as disciplined hands picked up the wolfskin
and tendered it to the hand with the lash.
This last was worse than the wolf.

II

Why was Mr Hyde worse than Dr Jekyll?
Those hairy greedy paws worse than manicured
    fingers
Writing prescriptions for hope?
That slouch and bent back more fierce
Than the worsted shoulders and hickory cane
Erect in slums whose sickness bends the just?

Housecalls to the pallid bored, discreet lifting of
    nightgowns,
The butler holding your hat, yawning porcelain
    teacups,
And then to the study, and gentleman's research.

If the weather is not too fierce, or the lunar rains too
    strong,
The man of conscience will then visit the poor.
In cellars and attics, on stained pallets,
Beyond gutters awash with a spew of poverty,
Where stink of lack flares fastidious nostrils,
The dying lie. They are meek before prestige.
The dark suit has the cut of power,
A valet at night takes off its smell of death.
Jekyll waives charges, yet what violence in
    prescriptions
Costing a week's wage, if wages were to be had.
In the dark of the moon these things leap out too
    clearly
Yet the physician defers rage, must walk soberly
    home.

O Hyde, the lash of conscience,
The teeth of knowledge, I love you.
You force Jekyll again into the streets,
To pad through filth and bare his real power.
He tears the girl drooping from the night shift,
And cuffs the workless drunk to sodden death.
The moon shows your work, you sit back on your
    haunches,
And smile and loll being at last yourself.
You are more truthful, a voracious fiction
Wolfing up all the lies of the humane.

III

In the last forest, wildness eluded maps
But not money. The trees had been
Rich in small beasts, and this had pleased the wolf.
He had run gently on leaves and fed on running
    things.

37

Trees were cleared, rock torn, cement and girders
    reared
A new kind of plant for another kind of growth.
Implacable things knocked out the sounds of power,
The forest went quiet and animals moved away.
The wolf slept, he stayed, his eyes in the leaves
Watched the order of men.
Hunger grew strong and he loped
A little nearer, to where people ate.
They threw stones, his leg dragged, perhaps
At the edge of the wood there was flesh running for
    him.
He came to the stop of trees. There was a road.
He ran on the road, and was hit. And the man
Controlling the steering, smiled,
Drew up stepped out and clubbed
The wolf to death.

Samson controlled the beast, cracked its jaws
For a last smile. He passed on
To deal with Philistines
While bees built in the skull.
Out of the strong came forth sweetness.

As you returned and smelt
Honey in those smiling jaws, you should
Have smelt sweetness despite yourself.
You killed the wild, turned the beastly to metaphor,
But you stink before the grace
Of wilderness. Run to the forest
And inhale the branching sound
Of original blood. Pace the roads,
Tear at your pride, suffer your own violence,
And beware wolves made as a smooth excuse.

2 iii 78

Finalities

There have been two leavings.
One morning I left, from the house you were
     losing,
When I returned both would be gone from me.
On a later evening, you walked from the house I
     rented.
Under the sign of transition, leaving confuses hope.
Both times were for crossing that painful sea
where difference is blurred but made entire
by a language shared only in misunderstanding.
The first time you moved under leaves
and flowers hung pink in a glassy urban morning.
Drowned and tentative, the watery northern
     summer
made ferns, lemon trees and the last champagne
share pale gold and green and general tears.
(Superstitious ancients poured the last for the Gods)
Your eyes greener than old turquies about your
     neck,
stones that change colour, to warn of ill to the
     absent,
you warned against going and delusions of change.

The second occasion was sharper,
more remote other meetings and places.
You were winter-brown, fur, and wool and leather.
You said: consider delusion, but jump. I only
said: now I have my voice; and fastened

blue lapis and pearls on your wrist.
You crossed the snow; it was as though the sea
had broken at my door and all my love
was ever to run across intractables.

I have carried your grief, silent and weak,
Have not sustained your courage. Have never
    spoken
The limits we shared. Verbose in most things,
I saw but loved you silently. My eye was too sure
To allow approximate words. How do we love
Those who know not to claim us?
Greatest giving is most hard to celebrate.
You shine beyond compliment, while my prosaic
    tongue
Stumbles on clumsy eulogy.
I have lived in delight of your house,
In the flowering clothes you have given,
In your light of intelligent sureness.
I too wished to give such pleasures, now fail even in
    praising:
Separation reveals you beyond all imitation.
You are brave as the sun, your doubts pure
    extremes as the snow;
be sure the doubts are to your lovers only
as intelligent gift, your love a quality
far beyond caution. Your eyes are clear summer and
    winter,
Your body brown leaves and green snow.
You have made more leavings and losses than I;
Simply, made and known more. Be sure, as I
Fudge the words, my heart inclines surely
To know what you were: simply, the best.

7 iii 78
21 ix 78

Their honesty

They both despised lies, and harshly asserted
Truth's monopoly, knew jesting Pilate's question
did not demand that they should stay for an
  answer.
He asked what truth is, while still not finding fault,
betrayed himself, knowing the question open;
so rash their sureness, it scorned the question
  down.
Their mouths like swords righteously blurted and
  sliced
the brains of muddled woolly sheep; they knew
  confusion and doubt should be dispersed by
  facts.
Supposed candour commanded each verbal
  mission:
Here, look, it is so, regard the glass I show you,
My quicksilver words block back your real image.
You are adulterous, ambitious, promiscuous fool
  or whore.
I am Mercury, divine message and sentence,
My mirror brings the definition you lack. Their
  words
betrayed their intelligence. They ran their mouths
with exact gabble of hyenas: the neat syntax,
preening cleanness of nouns, laughed as they ate
  things up.

Once, I fell between the two, a kind of tentative air

Crashed for sheer noise between their sounding
  cymbals.
One wielded preterite truths, soon in the present
Thrown back by the other's unreflecting sureness.
Between sword and glass another truth was broken.
They excised doubt, fractured older vaguer
  meaning,
Their confident words left only lie by excision.
Righteousness brought not truth, but merely a
  sword.

26 iii 78
8 iv 78
28 ix 78

A Garden Shut Up

The air is hot, breathed in the wings of insects,
the leaves turn stirring the smell of grass
cut green and rising. The poppies blow
under my hands and the sun slips and throbs
in the spreading hollows of mouth and knuckles and
    legs.
Lying, quiet, the lake of day
is moving and opening, the aimless intent
of afternoon green as a willow
hot as a bee.
                  On the other side
of the fence, you walk, and the snow falls.
It is terrible to see those sharp stars
fall on your hair and hands and your fierce
    shoulders,
icing the darkness.
                     This has to be met.
You do not waver, facing across
the trackless flattening field and narrowed
your eye on the bitter ridge of the wind
and steadfast your mouth to the air and the dark.

Walking walking I see you go in that place.
I cry out. The sound remains here
as noise of the willows, the legs of the insects,
the sun: to you it sounds as wind biting and cold
tears of the snow, each flake distinct
yet only perceived as coming against you.

I am trapped and held to watching,
a voyeur to defensive courage
facing its own fears. This pastoral voice
cannot cross to the wintry field without
becoming invasion. From grasses and willows
a cry rises like mist and meets the stare of the north.
You brush the snow from your face.

7 v 78

The horseman remembers

We hung, a single line of horses,
under the flank of the ridge.
In thin wind, the grating of larks,
the ringing of bridles, the wheeze
of horses, were all pitched
on the one high note. When we heard the scout
say we could ride, we did.
The plain falling out of the height
had grass ridged with poppies,
level as rock. Silver and red
dissolved to each other and we reached
the men we should kill. The meseta
ran behind us to shadow the arms raised
and the swords down, and blood and
white flesh and steel were the same.
I rode, and heard, and wounded a day
all things became like. Memory now
reminds that fear is not in the act
but in such seeing alike. I hear larks,
quite clearly, but hear swords beneath
and the hooves of the poppies and
sound of rock and of flesh. Courage is now
not in doing the separate thing
but in living with sameness.
Over the plain, in the wind,
under the saddle, riding the sword,
I learnt the fear of reduction.

Now when I hear larks I see blood
and death is that sound of the wind
white and level and plain.

6 vi 78
22 viii 78

Closed Order

The convent fronted the square, a pale façade
aloof to the noise and horses and crossings
of passionate feet. Bricked windows
were not supercilious, but final. Looking up,
there was wonder and fear in hearing it
said: a Closed Order. We knew
that meant, they never came out, save dead.
Even lay servants carrying bread
were scanned through the Judas window
before the door opened a body's width,
and the bread carnal from the oven
cooled as it passed that dark sill.

Next door, we borrowed dimensions of silence,
order and closure alien to our living. Mute,
the questions hung behind toys and dinners:
How do they do, with nothing of what we have?
How can they? How weird, dropping your own
     freedom
like cut hair, or papers blowing around the square.

One day at siesta I climbed
past drying sheets on the roof
up to the cistern and then
to the final tiles of the tower.
There was no space beyond heat,
it impaled all colour and sound,
each horse in bridle and shafts,

the breath of the world was stopped;
when sudden and subtle, meridian broke
in raining notes, the patter of palms
and of strings: so I saw rustling
below and screened, on their roof, five nuns.
One played the guitar and four
were dancing sevillanas. Black habits fell
away from unorthodox arms and innocent
smiles met in candescent pleasure.
Faces so pale, I had thought,
were supposed to be penitential.
Leaning, curving, they courted their sisters
with that dance, of the flesh, but in their order
they made it another thing.
The black skirts eddied and swirled
the glittering tiles of the floor, and the sun took up
their faces engraved in light.
For an hour, or two, or till night remade time,
I could not but watch, and even a boy
was ashamed to spy on such franchise.
Once down from the height I kept silent.

Years now, crossing other squares
and climbing up other towers, trying
to talk of freedom, and harder its finding,
I am still disturbed by that closed order
where, perfectly free, the daughters of God,
in open eye of the sun were calmly dancing.

19 vi 78
26 ix 78

For Henry Reed

In blind and bloody fighting
the enemy is not to be looked at.
That is Rule 1 of the Manual,
'Hand-To-Hand Fighting'.
That is, watch the movements,
divine the intentions, duck
the covert sureness going for your jugular.
Do not look at the face, the colour,
the presence. Rule 2 is, forget
why the enemy is the enemy.
Rule 3 is remember, attack, and
better, kill. The moves of aggression
usually show the enemy's confidence,
that is, their weakness. As they boast
youth, remember the fontanelle, and hit
(downwards, be precise, do not waste
on bruising). As they bully with success
remember vanity – allow the sneer
to say the success is scarce as they see it.
The sidewise attack of pathos is most
        treacherous but:
refuse their martyrdoms, disallow their history.
A sharp upwards blow on the right wrist would
suggest the victim was really an aggressor.
Harry with their own delusions. Do not
look at the enemy. Repeat; do not consider
those eloquent eyes, the softness of neck, the turn
of hair. That might undo just rage, unknit

escape, and in one second's
visceral turn to the particular,
lose all advantage to the
dread deceptive loved and cozening body –
the enemy who, most surely,
demands your attention only to have
out the guts of weakness
dislocate the bones of care,
and have you, then, onto the heap
of their own past refusals.

Do not look at the enemy.
Watch the movements.
Fascination brought you to this fight.
Now, at the end, be cool, and kill.
It is no policy to love where seeing's feared.
Your looking made you the enemy. Do not look.

vii 78

Woman falling

I saw her winding heavily
along the darkening curb, then,
looking back in the mirror, fallen
in the threading lines of cars.
We stopped to retrieve her.
She had canvas shoes and neat
patched trousers and dark wool coat
and the deadly methodical air
of the irretrievably drunk. On her face,
her terrible face, the old black eye
and the new buff blood. She had pride
sufficient to speak of walking into a door
and not mention exasperate fists. They said
she lived just near here.
Refusing a traceable name,
she gave it simply. Jane.

The army medic, stopped too from concern,
asked, How much have you had to drink?
then, Have you been to A. A.?
Alphas of cure; anonymity disallows
an omega of change. And his mate
called an ambulance, their C. O. to say they'd be late.
Her weight was against my side, her black gaze
accused reassurance. She said she was not going, not
anywhere in an ambulance. Her son,

only ten, was waiting. Refusal, last attack,
on the overbearingly kind. The medic
had dealt a lot with cases like this. He had?
for to: What do you do? came heavy-tongued reply:
I wind – I wind – wind – wind – *Braid*.
Imagine your days spent, coiling up decorative stuff
into rigid saleable form. There is no
dealing with that.
Her man did probably hit out
and the child was perhaps a weight
and she was the one poured the drink;
those aren't the case, but that braid.
Stitch stitch stitch, poverty, hunger, dirt,
we imagine such things are cured
there is an ambulance to come
but since none will unloose the chains
of binding, boring work, she had
Nothing to lose but herself.
It's still the Song of the Shirt.

II

Drunken despairing Jane, crazy Jane
not at all, crouched on some city curb,
patronized by a medical man in a naked public way.
Since we all, when we know we are trapped
execute that double bind, attack that which bears us
        down
by bearing down on ourselves, it's mere Samaritan
        oil
to call you: self-destructive.

And lucky, literary Lady Lazarus, writing how
Dying is an art, like everything else,
Which you do exceptionally well,

Let us now consider the unexceptional
The laborious, artless life;
Let us mark the social odds: if revenge of the weak
Is ever undoing their lives, articulate self-destruc-
     tion
At least revives other power. Under the palace of
     Minos
Let us see other daughters, in voiceless ordinary
     darkness,
Who thread without clew the reiterate labyrinth's
     needs.
Let us now consider those in the grave of the world
Whom the tongue of myth does not resurrect
On the third or the thirtieth day or any other.

                                        20, 28 ix 78

Progress of wisdom

They say that in absence fondness grows in the
   heart,
and that in the familiar breeds contempt.
I have found this true for my part.

They say what is unseen the heart can not grieve
   over,
and that unknowing ignorance is bliss.
This too I find true, divided from my lover.

Affection grows stronger, gone the feverish
   contempt,
there is no grief, not seeing familiar battles.
I forget the strain of building, and what that pain
   meant.

Harder rocks of the present, a growing city's
   bones,
with weathering time assume a simple grace.
Archaeologists measure, a mason hauls dirty
   stones.

I measured, fondly detached, that grand intract-
   able ruin,
coarse abandoned time, when our fingers were
   bloody for weeks.
And now want only making a place to live in.

The proverbs are true, but corrupt with easy
    thought.
The happy scholar is ignorant of the fighting,
the citizen's rowdy force while the houses were
    built,
is absent too from their living. This, division
    taught.
I am not fond of relics, of mere historical siting;
the living stones grow up as masons' blood is spilt.

This there is no saying in neat proverbial art:
contemptible, loving, grievous,
it's the present constructs the heart.

                                        28 ix 78

Reader

All day in clear sun flew the bird,
a considering eye bright
on the crisp things,
caught them, set them down
in the nestling's gape.

      Look, the light, a clear blue hollow, holds.
      The falling leaves are red,
      Sun curls late butterflies.
      I am pragmatic, I give you
      leaf, wing, lip under that light.
      But you my reader are
      always idealist, your eyes glue
      onto my details, your mind sucks
      my particulars, discards them,
      turns to your terrible pleasure
      in other, general, all.

The subject seen is sweet,
but that unseen is sweeter.
I would catch words whose substance
has no here but otherwhere;
then, reading, you could take
only echoed pleasure, beyond this murder
of bearer, winged or feathered.
I cannot write beyond
loved, needed things, cannot

escape in needed vaguer air.
Your free greed kills my needs.

      The sky one sees is blue and the tree
      rocks its branch. I am exact glutton
      for leaf and light and you,
      but you seizing my word
      refuse me and its lust. I desire
      things, your having them.
      You desire me as food,
      an augury of your life
      drawn from the entrails,
      suck out prophesy
      beyond things themselves.

I am corrupt in the test
those things best loved
become the fouled nest
in which your joy
is to pass out, pass on
the very thing, the toy my care
caught as winged itself, gone
into the gullet of oblique digestion.
Trapping that bud, snapping that wing,
I offer them up, and know
you swallow fair prey,
and reading, coming hard and sharp
on my details, grow and sing
your own song, your freed and general way.

                             17 x 78
                             22 i 79

Ballad for a Fair Lady

My father's gift was a black stone
Its heavy heart to shine as jet
And privilege impressed my bone
With map and compass steady set.

My mother's gift, a steely blade
To bend and curve and yet to kill
My sisters placed beneath my tongue
The bleeding fires that burn it still.

So Mirror, shining conscience,
And Blade, the pliant commonsense,
The decorous Map, rebelling Blood,
Were four great gifts to do me good.

I walked the world and bent a while,
Killed fear with common compromise,
And with my class's taste for style
Politely mapped the many lies.

But in the mirror of my heart
The blackest truths shone sharp and clear,
That made me sing, and coarse the songs,
Then blood washed clean my tongue from fear.

It flowed onto the Map and burned
The decorous roads that I had learned.

I ran and threw away the Sword
And black and stony shone my word:

> Now, in the fire and in the flood
> Beware that not all gifts are good.

18 i 79
22 i 79

Going to sleep with your rings on

Have you noticed, if you go to sleep with your
    rings on
your knuckles swell, and the skin devours the
    metals?
The gazelles you put into the painting because
    they were pretty
turn and devour the leopards and then the paint-
    ing
eats up the pavilions where it was passed from
    hand to hand.

The ring with clasped hands your hero gave you
but then it was stolen, your heroine gave you
    another
save those hands held a heart that was crowned.
He was a radical historian, she a princess writing
the history of all the gazelles who painted their
    own picture.

The Navajo silver and turquoise was given you
    on your birthday
by the woman who later became your worst
    enemy.
You wear it under the knuckle with plastic rings
    on each side
they eat up the hate but it's odd that it matches
the double coral your lover bought in the rainy
    pavilions.

I have noticed in sleep my hands are painting
     pictures
passing gold and silver and coral in rings round my
     enemies
and also my lovers whose many valuable gifts
would be a history of decoration were it not they
     held in common
the radical bone, left in the burnt-out pavilions
for the leopards to smell while gazelles graze in the
     rain.

for Bradford Stark   23 i 79

The Aerial Years

O come all young people/and list while I sing
The love of your place/is a terrible thing
For banishing fear/and encouraging pride
Be constant to move/with a whore's common
    stride

Those were the years I took planes. Constantly
Constantly waiting in airports, for taxis and buses
Bleached voices making announcements
for Tehran, Philadelphia, London, Munich
                                    Endlessly
Cities up on the screens and endlessly
gathering bags, cameras and whisky, I went
Constant only in signs of willed displacement
to and from cities of war, broken pacts
conventions of brotherly love.

Once in the air and tempest
on an island below stood the ruler
king of the place, conjuring down
with his wand, the common fears of air
to be still in the earth and the book of rules
in his hand. Mud lapped his monstrous ankles
fire spelled his book away.

They were also the years I learned to love women
constant in needing to move, to get
the hell out, to sign in the air

their treaties of fire. Lamenting
my books, my pots, my cat, I broke
the solid sorceries. Disowning
I burnt my books and ended
free of the rule, the wand of the muddy monster
of earth, in earth; made pact with our displacement.

In an airport, once I remembered
from another convention, the rigid rule:
Ladies don't move, while I was moving
two thousand miles east, which I thought
    suggested
the common women do. Not even owning
the mud they walk on, it cannot keep them
flying against the sun, setting their movements
revolutions of fire, over still, powerful monsters.

Terror of loss, of being
displaced, footloose, rootless, the boredom
at moving squalor, are nothing
beside constancy in air, fire, power.
Planing the grains of earth
air is a screen to show
remotely yet, cities of concord.
The air uprooted makes
for spelling the place, the constant
escape from islands, bleached wings rotten in mud.

And those were the years I thought I might see
a more prosperous time getting the heaven out.

                                            24 i 79
                                             1 ii 79

Sonnet for Shakespeare, Woolf, and Others

It must be said lastly of love
That no set genes engender it,
And here I am now set to prove
What to all poets has seemed fit:
That male plus female only is a norm
That barters content for the sake of form.
I am too much a sensualist
Not to love women, and too intellectual
Not to love men, and I have wished
This weren't construed as something merely
    sexual.
We all desire the Other and we should
Think in the Self, there corporate wisdom's laid.
I'd have men love men's bodies if I could,
And women women's, that wise flesh be made;
And have us stretch, sensing our minds to change,
To what is common and to what is strange.

I ii 79

Against Yeats

O dear wonderful humbug
spouting your ceremonies
of innocence, while you
imagined yourself a swan,
all the genteel porn of
the classical painters
helping you to imagine
yourself with a great, big
bill beating above that girl.
Wondering if, *mastered*, (revealing
pun) by your brute blood,
Leda contrived to put on
your knowledge, as she got
the sharp point of your power?
All power just is that,
revealing indifference to
knowledge of those mastered.
Yet I take some delight in it all,
the great dictator telling
his secretary his nights
out he's a feathered glory,
as he slides the swan skin out
of his desk. I've heard with delight
several professors slide out
this poem as vision of history:
the father of the gods
engendering Troy and all that
by poetic justice of rape,

and the breeding ground of it all,
history lounging there, vague
fingers pushing across
the page. You imagined
the swan a holy dove, a violent
annunciation, yet can't quite save
yourself from compromising analogy,
a Holy Ghost that looks like Papageno.
Inexpressible silliness, but you
expressed just that, the great
unpaid bill, history lately
falling about in laughter as
putting on swan-suit you
are caught with your trousers down.

4 ii 79

Mrs Pinkerton, widow of
Admiral Pinkerton, U.S.N.

The lieutenant's wife is in the garden
waiting, her pink and white linen
crumpled by alien heat. Pink and white
prodigal plum blossom falls on her jacket,
kid slippers. Through the screens,
in the house, she can see great branches,
blossom placed in porcelain jars on the floor,
already falling, waxy silt on the wood.
Extravagant, flowers where you cannot afford
ordinary dressers and chairs. Black butterflies
flick and dip swallow tails in the heat.
She remembers a funeral, her mother's
midwestern voice: A lady is always
a lady, even when things are bad.
It does not occur she should fear
waiting, knowing her rights. This is
a last act, tidying the parlor after
the mourners leave. She flicks petals
from her pin-tucks. Abruptly she sees
a Japanese woman skim the terrace,
black and gold silk jutting around her.
The woman looks at her and raises one hand,
it says: wait. This is a different waiting,
her heart knocks, the sweat runs in her slippers;
she thinks, *sorrow*, then *I never did
think that word*, then *a real lady*,
then *now, I know how things are bad.*

The lieutenant's wife is in the garden.
In the house something heavy falls to the floor.
There is one cry, stones fall on her
shoulders, it is her husband's voice
but she thinks, *he is not my husband*.
The butterflies are black bats,
and she covers her ears.
The lieutenant is standing in his uniform
white against the screens, his hands on the child
who is wearing black.
The three of them walk away
but not together, not in the garden
or ever.

        Decades later, an old lady hears
that the opera is banned:
America is at war with Japan,
the camps in Idaho are full,
and *Butterfly* is 'pro-Japanese'.
Darn right, she snorts, having
learnt in the garden a harder
language she never spoke to
the husband. Her son comes in
through the screens. He smiles. He has
slanted eyes. They turn off the wireless
and put Puccini on the gramophone.
He lays his hands on her shoulders
and pink dogwood in her lap.
Not quite the music's allegiance
but a flowering into truth.

27 iii 79

Things moved are, usually, better

Things moved are, usually, better.
Like earth ploughed and smelling and shaped
brown and sweet, and the sidewise mouth of the
    child
moving and smelling, feeding, the new and the
    soft.
And also the branch shook in the wind
revealing a sun the midday eyes had not known
or seen for that matter. Indeed even the
comet tail of the plane is better than just
the plane; it is numbered among movements
of stars, and not merely as flight.

But what of the heart? It too is a thing.
If it were not to open and close, to move
we too could not see, movement, or any thing
turning or stirring or sucking or given
the odd and beautiful life of the moved.
Yet as it moves and knocks and now my tongue
moves in a figure, it is not better.
It is sour and bitter and smells as if sky
were not there and is numbered as fear.
It's a fault in the heart it moves not merely as
    thing.

Harvey, you showed King Charles how the
    valves pumped
and moved the heart, discovered a figure of life,

remaking all medieval romance had seen
as a figure for feeling. Feeling feeding on life
is the moving thing, not perhaps life as it moves.
Earth and flesh moving, forgive us this fear.

16 iv 79

Conjunction

At night, when the ward was more or less quiet,
she sat writing a letter.
It was a cold winter and most of the patients were
   dying.
The young were away at the war, or else in hiding.
The lamp was shaded, the light golden.
She wore a long grey cotton dress
and yellow hair drawn to her neck.
It was a love letter.

After the cries, complaints, demands
were comforted, she would write:
'I think of your voice when you speak
laughing, or sing. Once you were
in the next room and I heard you
talk to the cat. I am so happy.'
He wondered how she could hear such sounds
above the whining summons, death rattles.

She changed dressings where the ward smelled
   thick;
gangrene. She soaked bandages off ruined skin.
'Your knees and shoulders are like wet stones,
the skin is so fine and taut. Horses run
under my hands as I touch it. When you were
digging, your back reflected the sun. I love you.'
He tried to think how it was she could see
wounds and pus, and also that supple glint.

The constant thing was the pans, all the liquids
viscous or stinking, seepage of bodies. She cleaned
   up,
washed her hands, and picked up her pen. 'I loved
the mornings we lay together, the sheets soaked
   beneath us,
and laughed and talked, and then bathed together.
I am smiling as I write this.'
He puzzled about her conjunctions
but was delighted to do so.

She amazed him, holding so much in eye and mind
and not distracted: she loved his body precisely,
where bodies were vast and monstrous.
She would not have seen this as paradox.

It is not clear which should be most admired:
she for imagining him, the exact form of their love,
while she worked with those in dissolution;
or he, for imagining her, trying to know how she
   wrote
in a place, among things, that he found only
   repulsive.

She finished the letter and sealed it
and wrote his name on the front.
Then stood up, put it in the pocket
of the grey cotton dress, and went to give it to him.
It is not important that he too had died
by the time she reached his bed.

15 vii 79

Travellers

In the green and brown of the atlas,
promising more than any travel brochure,
lay the facts of contour, tide and height.
They saw how the city was set
armed by hills and the river running
from the Roman towers north to
the washed beaches south. They said
they would go to the city, be held
by hill, cooled by water sung over
by winds from snow or sand.

They settled in for the land of optimism,
months of fact. Despair to fall off,
and uncertainty too and no neighbours
or friends to blur corners or lines of truth.
There was no fact beyond the facts of body.
And there at last was insupportable mass.
No continuing city; all abiding, impossibility;
mountainous illusions shadowed the delta.
They said they must flee the city;
but each time you pack, the heart
is a smaller box, the tickets
cost more. Singing we go to the city
and leave with laments for other
yet other delusions. The atlas
does not lie, but we do.

At the frontier, the customs
opened their cases, and the stench clouded

the hall. They held their gloves
to their nose, seized the contents,
confiscated the cities, packed seventeen
deep. Schliemann would have honoured
such impacted wreck, but not
I. I found there the face
of Agamemnon. They carried the cities
sieged in hope, taken lightly,
demolished brutally, then abandoned,
but no memorials save chiselled
fear. The gold was there
under countries *en transis*:
an atlas clean and glossy
below the rotten lay of
their land. The officials politely
judged they might keep it,
but phoned ahead to the next border,
alerting their colleagues
of further depredations.

iii 79
8 iv 79

The oldest tale

In the pub, a little after opening-time,
morning sun gold on slopped glass-rings,
the night's remains, a few flies
spittling the shining rounds, dried sugar:
and three young men were whiskering up
the hair of the dog. Their eyes hung
stupidly over mouths without habit of life;
and they supped up the second round.
Hot, rooting, the alcohol loudened the boasts
just as the hearse slid by. Black lacquer
darkened, for a minute, the windows
and the eyes and the glasses blanked.
Jocular, contemptuous in questioning
who it was, poor fool corpse
eyes waxed close under shut lid
and waxy wreaths, but the publican's answer:
Your friend, shut them up for a second.
In the habit of war and killing it surprised
them to learn he'd been got by Death.

> I mean, dead, our age, well somebody
> Got him, so we don't know this
> Death, we ought to find the bugger.

They swayed out, the streets closed away
under the gun-points, no one to ask
but the old man who didn't much care
about danger, dying, or for them.

> Ah, Death, death, he said, softly
> I've searched and longed and lusted that

So long. Late and morning now
How my stick taps these tripping cobbles
Knocking and asking that earth
That motherly levelling fall of the lot of us
To let me in, but – (jostling now)
Bloody old fool, bet he's Death's scab,
Those young sharp fingers gripped and shook
his smile from him, the sudden smile of malice:
Are you seeing that tree? Down that little
Twist of a path, by the factory, the
sprouting
Protestant churchyard? Well, there, you'll
find –
And running they saw under the roots, the coins
the sliding mounding fall of gold and silver,
a shining pile of old desire and habit:
No longer then after Death they sought.
They saw what they'd always seen,
spoils, the easy killing, winning where others
earned.

[undated]

Burnt we do burne

There is fire in the streets
and licking the suburbs.
The men came to fight us
and the tall mad one in front
had a riot shield blood fiery red
and on it: Burnt I do burn.

Burned we learnt to burn
books and houses,
and like the widows of Samothrace
to throw children into flames
and then ourselves, and invaders
cannot see the letters:
Burned, we do burn.

We took the shield from his corpse.
We needed it, fending off scalding
hate. Shapes of our homes
and our children's bodies
were described in flames.
Burned our air shaped how we burn.

We do not speak of emblems of redress.
The sickle cannot cut corn where
the foxes with tails tied together
run flaming. No hammers beat out
the words: burnt we do burn.

Rage can only borrow fire, possible
art: assume we might not be clay.

Clay does not burn and
silt easily makes fertile
shapes on the plain, shielding
us from fired forests. But I and my
friends run with shields through flickering
    branches.
Burnt, we do burn.

14 ix 79

The poetry competition

The stipulation:
no submission should
exceed thirty
two lines in length.

Now where was the point
the measure of that? The year
before Dante walked *nel mezzo
del cammin*? or before the Baptist
came from the desert
for the demands of A.D. 33?

At thirty two we have mostly resigned
the poem of time and chance,
length of remaining
unfilled space appals us.

The 32nd parallel runs through Savannah,
Nanking, Tucson, and Ciudad Juarez,
and Isfahan, where the streets are now grey
with dust, the grains counting how far they
are from Tucson. To the south, in Rio Grande
a poet sends a telegram epic to Kalgoorlie
which is not understood as it passes north
of Santiago and Buenos Aires. The response,
two dusty sestinas along the same parallel
not in the English language.

The search for a reason
goes to the danger of history,
exotic symbolic places; returns defeated
to dry desert safety having
only the measure of things. Ageing,
our memories are neat and selective
but won't stomach argument, won't take the
    chance
of the sprawling time we loved discourse more than
    an image.

31 X 79

Self-murder through silk

Sending bright silk to his
soft flesh, she planned a
marrying gift. A shirt,
the shirt of Nessus, his anger
made it stick. Jealousy ran in
threads' soft sticky burn, a
jelly glued on the veins. His
science of distortion powered him
his death. All blood and knowing
past were gifts in love to him
but to him enemy blood.

Into this mud-hot lie
she could not wade, or weave
even an attempt at jealousy.

Delight stopped up
and charred trees
his colonies. The fact that
cloth came via others burned
his eyes and pores, to what
was hers to give, a truth.
To be possessed the land
and past should burn, the possessor
cinder. He thought the gift
an aerial picture of
submission; threads shining
a warp of rivers he could dam

at will, tracks he alone cut.
Gold flares sighted
his triumphal entry.

The map she sent was for
joint journey, not campaign.
She'd consulted earlier
geographers, historians,
weavers. But what was known
in silk unrolled to fire
skin, stuck and stuck
on his victorious sense.

Tearing hell from the fabric
Hercules wept his
new-found land. *Chi fu?*
Chi fu? – Nessuno, io stesso –
O mentitrice, io, l'uccisi.
Called her liar
even in claiming killing, gave
his own throat a present
to burning jealous now.

She is calm as his tomb.
Deianeira has abandoned gifts
is instructed in closeness.
She will not weep nor
Desdemona lie any more
under worn strawberry shrouds.
But the fatigues are deadly.
The sons of heroes seize
still on their fathers' shirts.

14–23 xi 79

82

Self-murder through silk
[Gay Clifford's note on the preceding poem]

Hercules the hero, husband of Deianeira, was notoriously unfaithful. Nessus tried to abduct Deianeira, so Hercules shot him. Dying, Nessus gave her a shirt soaked in his blood, saying it had power to make Hercules love her truly. She sent it to Hercules to wear at one of his victory celebrations, hoping to revive their love. But the shirt burned Hercules to death and he died cursing Deianeira.

Otello, the brilliant mercenary, wrongly imagined Desdemona had been unfaithful, so he throttled her in bed. As she died, her maid asked who had killed her; she protected Otello by saying 'No one, I myself'. He denounced her as a liar and then killed himself.

14–23 xi 79

83

For the memory of Bradford
Stark, poet, 1948–79

On this shelf: porcelain
Chinese maybe 1520
its maker dead
pale simple provenance
irrelevant. It steadies the whole room.

The talk of poets may be
a strange glazed box,
Céladon green as no water
with the shadow of ash,
called for the colour of an actor's cloak,
Céladon the lover, rejected, comic and empty,
and in it faintly cracks
and shimmers shape our hearing.
When we write to each other
postcards or poems the box
is loaded not with its value
but with how we know
what is under the lid.

The glaze elusive,
the colour anonymous
that space empty –
say inheritors: what is it?
collectors: we must buy.
It stays wrapped in old papers
or on show, with silk and lights.

But we never owned either the box or its uses,
only knowing each other knew what it held:
cracks of firing, green of intense invention
and a sound, like the talk of women
(we children under the box of the table)
saying terrible things, how we come to be born and
    die,
knees steady, while they gossiped and pared our
    food.
What we spoke to each other echoed out of their
    facts.
No room for play, our poet-noise
muffled and cloaked, shape of the unsaid,
a slight hum making known fear
of their discards fuelling the kiln.

19 vi–x 80

Virginia; the Old Dominion

Imagine, as a European,
honeysuckle as hostile.
The Jewish Professor, his wife Italian,
when he moved from New York
bought and planted honeysuckle.
Virginians laughed at
coals to natural Newcastle.

A scented kudzoo, it climbs
smells and kills. Here
two years are enough for arms
tough and dry as Anchises'
clamped on his son's neck
humping out of flaming Troy
to rewind us in dead maples
and locusts. Each Spring
fleshy sinews house tent-caterpillars
which drop on your hands
when you burn them with kerosene.

Virginia, a kind of parkland
deceives eyes used to
grazing-lines and grassland.
Step across fences and the praying
mantis, a fertile protestant
unction eating your sense
of amicable neatness, waits:
watches the poke-weed, its mock grapes
squished in the shit of robins,
not robin really but a red thrush

named for nostalgia to fend off the alien,
and her children swarm
across crab-grass and locusts and
tulip-poplars; Napoleon's northern roads
could not be lined with things
that shudder with orange
vertical blossoms. And dogwood
and magnolia are hot and white
as cherry is not. Dogwood, locust
crab-grass, eating and pinching
creatures harry these names.

Capability Brown, what would you?
the state is deceptive, state of the virgin
queen but really an old politic whore
in a robin-red wig.
Pretence of innocence, starting afresh,
an old country calls your things
by natural names of power,
hangs round your neck the menace
which gardens of England
say is gone.

The Jewish professor dreams.
The box and gravel of Florence
are covered with spores
from new-world parkland,
crunched by small mandibles;
the novice hooker's myth,
new life away from old power.
Escaped from fires,
the green and pleasant
meets old greedy menace.
Waiting honeysuckles
dogwood crabgrass locusts.

7 x 80

87

[Untitled]

My house is on a cliff; that it should fall
was what I thought when agents showed each wall.
But that it's I that dropped I never dreamed.

Through each glass dependent views I'd call
and saw the sand run and the water creamed
into strange peaks streamed to no land at all.

I think the drop first made me hear, as beamed,
that wireless message from the seismic hall
where they had measured future scales of shock
and thought to warn us from the hanging rock,
but my own falling mass knew as it dreamed
that I could not avoid the drop at all.

Emprisoned in the winds beyond the wall
we plunge and gorge where all the furies lean
Buying a house did not mean this at all.

8 xi 80

Confession

My ghostly Mother, I me confess
I've been indecent, more or less.
Lapses of courage are always indecent.

You had a greyer time, in which was lent
The social ways to lie. It was not meant
That you should say exactly what you miss.

It seems to me that I was always bent
Doing the things were safely social, meant
To block the questions are without redress.

But now I dread old fears that cannot press
Out into pleasure, where cowardice is rent.
My ghostly Mother. I do confess.

Lapses of courage most reveal our bent
The ways we will not say who tears our tent
The bear who rips and then demands a kiss.

But all you missed in decency I'm sent
To say should now be asked for, and the rent
In nature of our loss I now confess.

We are not silent, and the tears are less.
I tore myself our pleasure to express.
We social ghosts could now say what we meant.
The bear's not there if we should strike our tent.

14 xii 80

89

Camping Out

The eye is a circle of fire
and in that circle
we may see beyond wolves
and perhaps, within, warmth.

Now there is only potlatch burning
gifts meant as honours
now the heat of fears.

As my eye burns I see the destruction of circles
and hear my lover say there is always the round.
The iris contains the dilations of pleasure,
the pupil always the constriction of fear.

You were my teacher; in the hurt of your shoulder
I learnt the iris can't shimmer lightly as skin.
I as the pupil saw extreme terror
and heard the wolf breaking the circle.

I stand in my eye and see how it loves
The ashes are raked and I see what it proves
The night and the baying are beyond sound
The warmth beyond feeling. The fire not in the
   ground.
Your shoulder aches, though it makes the burning.
I am still in the ashes. A kind of learning.

In the circle of fire the eye sees that it may
Destroy the circle, and blindly throw things away.

for D.T.D.   3 i 81

From Eurydice

O take but pity on us here
and only let us sleep
for we must ever answer you
each time we hear you weep.

And take what pleasure while you may
and in the world rejoice
for here there is no space for play
nor any human voice.

You were the first I ever loved
the last I ever saw
but here I find that it is proved
you may not hurt me more.

Then ride and race above the earth
among the winds and free
for you shall find there's nothing worth
when you shall lie with me.

For you will come in all your grace
within this narrow gate
and find at last your own space
when it is all too late.

We lie here in the dead cold clay
yet do not think we grieve,
for harder face the light of day
than care not what you leave.

There is no staying there my sweet
for all who ride or go.
We come at last an earth to meet
and loving do not know.

The wind does blow tonight my love
your voices in the rain,
so make yourself content my love
they will not call again.

19 iii 81

An Interview While Writing
a Biography

'. . . and then also the man who did not even like
   dolphins.
Taking the ship to Genoa, stunned blue about us,
the top deck was bare, most of the passengers
milled in the handkerchief pool, the girls as bad as
   topless
(given their tops) determinedly ground on their
   stomachs,
straps undone for getting a dorsal bronze.
Then, cutting the blur over water,
nosing up and into water from air
those amazing beasts started teasing around us.'

She didn't notice she cried
telling me, and said:
'I told him I'd laughed when – I must
have been four or five – I saw them
first from the troop-ship going to my father,
I think I'd got the measles, so went on deck
when the rest were eating, and my mother –
no, was it? perhaps a sailor – said
a school of dolphins, and I wanted
to go to school. They are magic, you know.
They flirt around with our ignorance, I mean
our ignoring of pleasure.' And then she was
silent, as the tape moved.

'I moved his eyes to them, and he
reached for his lenses – I stopped him

from choosing, leant towards him, I suppose
I jiggled the camera, laughing to those
loony backs, a sort of un-gunned salute
– like a grin in motion but graceful.
Perhaps I never loved anybody as much
as then, but –'

Her voice trailed, the machine went,
the sun was wannish over her clutter;
that kind of sadness that's not expression
but built knowledge on loss.

'We make a mistake, thinking the world
loves us. To know one is happy isn't
to give it to others. Do you know what he said?
Just, *they're a kind of mammal*.
He was right of course – he mostly was –
but not delighted. You talk to me
as a writer: how can I be that
if on that June ship I couldn't transmit
the error of happiness?

Could we stop? I am tired, now.'

That's the last time I was with her,
except for her sea-side burial,
and it seemed the interview
that said the most.
I record it but can't to this day
say, why that tape is blank.

3 v 81

Never again as we were

Going back: the hardest,
assuming shapes, trees, tongues
imagined we once had.

Foligno riding, his checker-board horse
on neat squared fields dressed small
expressing ill-will
from Siena to Florence, their different shields.
Sharp hills, unsentimental trees,
olives hacked bare in March,
naked reversed Daphnes, weeping
to make our delicacies.
And always cypress, sporadic pointing
grammatically giving the eye
a pleasure of order,
its kind of stature outgrowing its own scale.

You went away, and away heard of the fire,
on the road to Siena, burning for ten days,
burning scrub, and oak and baring bones
of landscape, you thought to be home –
im Eland, im Ausland –
there they were burning each other
but at home too soon they start firing.
And then the worst, to natural Romantic cant,
the cypresses started dying,
splayed, and browned, and looked deeply untidy.

To look on disorderly landscape,
which doesn't smell, an alien vulgate
of competition, makes you wonder
why supposed unstriven delight
should be so missed, or subtle
conflicting scents, bark and fruit, be a need
(*im Elend, im Ausland*).

Deciding to go again
you know can strip you bare,
re-root in knowing
exactly how little you know.
The olives make grey and silver, still
you could drive in mist to serene
shielded Siena. But in the cypress
ruined inside, its heights unsinged,
shedding itself, no longer pandering taste,
there is that which roots desire
— *in a familiar land, the strangest love.*

To be away, go foreign,
to lose aim of place —
can't be dread or regret
in memory of cypress,
where dark height has no shadow
and undoing contains itself.

3 v 81

Secret heroine from
Joseph Conrad

She went out on the streets, faced facts of war,
picked herself through rubble, wondered it seemed
    far
going to work on broken bricks, the new ruined
    town.
She'd been at Taylor Woodrow, now worked
    further down
across the main road, the place where they made
    arms.
Somehow construction work was no different from
    munitions.
Her employer about the same, she accepted old
    conditions.
He did not even need the grace to see any harm
the morning she came in in tears, did not take her
    hand,
but she cried over the new designs, and about the
    fighting,
drafted mistakes in the model, under inadequate
    lighting.
We got to test it, and the pit replaced the land.
Our own people fell in, and we minuted alarm.

I'm haunted still and still don't love her less.
She drew the detail wrong, but knew the real mess.

When the pit gapes and all the idols fall
When every icon's shaken from its wall

When every birth must simply be aborted
When all our bravery's gone or been distorted
We could remember just who built those walls
And not ignore ourselves who dug the pit.
In our conceptions we construct ourselves
And Gods we make, may be appalled by it.

23 v 81
2 vi 81

Cats and all

It has to be said first that all the best lovers
Love cats. Perhaps it's their tact, perhaps it's
Their grace, perhaps the fact that cats
Have the art of being stupid but always a pleasure.
Possibly, too, that they know when to stay
Allow themselves a small space on the bed
When the hurt is worst; and also when to go —
The quiet small asking to leave at six
When they have their other affairs, and know
You have yours as well. In the dark nights
No lover of cats imagines they're all the same
Grey. They shine and are brilliant at being
Exactly what we should want to see and feel.
I hope if I lack a lover, leaving this world,
I might have a cat to tactfully lead me through
The difficult business of losing and going,
With charm and enough grace to be fierce;
With the claws in, though the eyes sharp.

for Christina Gascoigne   10 vi 81

I will consider my cat Thisbe

I will consider my cat Thisbe —
She possesses more years in account than mine
And I fear does not fear the Lord.
She is indeed of the tribe of Tyger
And has been known to be in the garden conversing
With Angels, when she would not eat them.
When she stretches her claws no heart can bribe her.
In light sun of the morning she lies with paws
    upwards.
In the dark of night she runs the carpets and thuds.
When I am sick at heart she lies quiet beside me
When I am in doubt her nose reassures me
When I am angry she stops being a Tyger
And, as the Lamb, tells me the Lord made me.
Then she is fierce and watches the wall to see
What Pyramus lion shall come through the hole to be
An enemy. Her whiskers possess great sweetness;
They curl downwards and when they drop I collect
    and keep them.
And the stripes of her tail are blacker than dark,
And her white bib and white paws are the mark
Of the cat who runs for the Tyger but knows the
    Lord
And who has the art of lying all over words.
To consider Thisbe is better than thinking of books.
How she stretches and knows to appear dull while
    she works.

7 iv 82

For Bisi, genius loci

On either side the poppies show
In clumps beneath the violets grow
The house is a slim brown ship
Out of rain on the hill.

Two white cats flump and slip
From grass to the door and into the ship
One gold and wounded, where the herbs are dry
The other earless, hunting, guards the hill.

In another country she wonders why
You should make lists until you die:
Rates, gas, mortgage, (not roses acer and jasmine)
These can corrupt the will.

In the mind's eye both are seen
The rain on the hill where the cats have been
The dead paper and bills and dust
The herbs, the ship, flower into her will.
On either side the yellow spikes –
Broom fresh to old hill.
Seth is in search for the oil
of grace.

18 v 84

Notes on the characters of men

This is a poem from grace and also of delight
and about the many reasons we need to love men.
There is the man who sleeps with his knees apart
– a curious innocent loving diagonal art.
And the man who can not chew a cob of corn
without washing his beard, or smell of butter gone;
has flown his fierce planes but when wounded
became a scholar. And also the man who loved
his mad mother, and went to be a great lawyer,
from Nottingham buses, and proved class didn't
    matter.
And the one who thought he was Byron but had the
    hair
that shone in meetings and blazed bureaucratized
    air.
And the one whose wife has a great and factual skill
in telling the world's hurts, but not always sees his
    own,
and he doesn't grudge, but sees she is setting down
in her own way what made him himself. And the
    one
who deeply betrayed could still laugh and delight
when she left the tables with winnings made that
    night.
And the man who died in Ireland, but then wasn't
    dead,
took trouble to ring months later, deny what papers
    said.

The man who fathers another's child, deep in
    professional skill,
pretending and aching where the legal would prove
    ill-will.
And the two dour Scots, who acted the boss with
    exigence
but given a chance could always give to vulnerable
    defence.

My life was made on their courage and beauty and
    dare:
Perhaps no longer important to write that I share
memory and the moving facts of their very selves —
we are lucky to have lovers, do not put them on
    shelves.
I am made in their grace and care, and cannot
    rescind
my admiring and love of the difficult life they lend
to me and my kind. And I will not undo that love.
Dear, blighted Pope — *no characters at all* — ?
My muse is greater, loving yours and all.

11 vi 81

Miriam and William

Guillermo Cabrera Infante y Miriam Gomez

In a house humming with birds
Where flowers blow down coral stems
Where crystal shoes run under crystal hair
There are two lives escaping words.

Beyond the windows are imagined prisons
And urban arches through the blackest brick
And they have seen them and avoided hurt
To show to others words their seasons.

It is not easy to be wise and good.
Nor facile to be funny, nor to stare
At arching prisons and see only hair.
In those like these all thought shall be a good.

18 vi 81

[Untitled]

Leaving a poet before the day was done
Is not a trick, but to see clouds like
Cliffs looming, note small crabs like stars
Bleached from an old tide on the grass,
Tide waters gone grave equal light.
You need cities, and to let them pass,
You need poets and to see them pass;
A voice to say it hears, to take you far
From every populous place and then make right
The going back to what you have to face;
An amber sun to make a hard-worked field
Be tolerance, love, and passing every fright,
Forget to do your face: a poet knows
In stars, in grass, or cities is repose.
Vision of grammar carries its own night.

21 vi 81

How, wild?

How wild is wild? came the wild wind crying
As I returned disguised to Ephesus.
Not for the town where they hold council,
Only to see the chaste and politic,
The goddess of denial who can give
Others disguise who come to Ephesus.

This road is blank said a wild wind crying
The city lighting shows up only dust
Disguises all the avid faces buying
Some path to anything to pass as trust.
Now in the dust and storm deliver us.
For I return, disguised, to Ephesus.

Powers don't hate when we must ask them things,
For this the way they show the power they have.
A wild demand against the fiercer fears
And scurry in a frightful dust that brings
Against the falseness claims delivers us.
Whipping our ears comes the wild wind and tears,
I am denied, but still delivered thus,
For in disguise I turn to Ephesus.

25 vi 81

Philomela's sister to her physician

None shall charge you with dullness if you see
The bird of night   on this blackened tree.
Do not forget Philomela had a sister
Not only savaged but her tongue cut out,
She wove a message that the sister read:
In the slaves' quarters, and then song broke out.
Tereus' bloody tongues   then transferred
To others' chanting   shouting   half un-dead
The swallow flies in circles   and is heard
Crying the knowledge cured, the violence fled.

Physicians came and metamorphosed pain
The birds fly out and don't remember pain
They cry and fly to Athens from the pain.

Remember healing is a changing art:
It's Procne we remember bringing summer wind,
And nightingales give love to what we   find
Under woods' blackness, for tongues were
     wrapped
In darkness,   ache,   and the unchanged trap
Before the doctor who could cull the web
Came and laid pain to bed and heard its heart.
Those ancient transformations   only part
The way the dark of winter makes some way
Into the airs of summer   the scent of hay,
The gods, the healers, changed those ravaged
     birds

To swallow,   hoopoe,   and their hurtful words
Into the quiet vengeance   light and day.

for Dr Preston   1 vii 81

[Untitled]

Here was the man who most regarded honour
but in himself no one could place their trust.
He was ferocious, that could not inhibit
those who loved him as they could and must.
In wild spaces his lame form inhabits
an honourable waste, a steamy place
in which the politics of passion race
trusting, untrusting, an unreliable saint.

We have no way to say how the fierce comes,
how the insuperable dishonest breeds
a clearer answer to our closest needs,
where we had thought that formal honour meant
to be our friend, and pallid truth had lent
some light to riot or to the still
hour when we see just how to kill
another's form of passion, their grace.
Telling the truth is not important;
ill are the shapes that come with varied cant
to say there's one truth, not another's will.

He willed his being and shall so survive.
The world is richer and he is alive.
He flew the angry and expensive jet,
knew how to make the sky yield space and yet
be blue, or calm, or full of angry cloud.
He never let his hurt cry out aloud.

I place no trust in him. But all my love
shall force the truth to yield that I shall give
a proof of honour where the best proofs live.

14 vii 81

Boating party

When sudden on the still lake rain falls —
you have seen it — the water blackens,
two elements become each other; it happens
that quiet is brought to noise by squalls
— the reeds bend and the oak is shook
and on the blackened surface, look,
roots seem to rise and say that hell
was on that surface that seemed smooth,
and smoke appears where was no fire.
The churning up is what we loathe.

We hate to see the still inspire
drowned air where we sailed so well,
the smooth jib bellied out, a lyre,
a triangle of white in sun
that hummed and pulled to our desire,
opposing shore, a different mud,
where reeds and oaks looked different.

These things don't ever come in towns:
the Serpentine is always black.
The pochards, Carolina ducks,
in Saint James' always have to sail
black oily water. Gardeners hack
weeds away along the shore.
The real drowning comes, you see,
where lakes dispose to fire and we
must sail and sail if rain has gone.

Water and air dispute themselves.
The reed and oak assume themselves.
The rain strikes on and on and we
a boating party, contest, what we see.

                                        12 vii 81

Something for Victor Jara:
vox populi

I was   other   that is why I cared
to find voice   or acts   shared
now am only   gaps   and blackness.
Victor Jara   they cut his hand
his fingers one & one & said: play.

And in the stadium of others' dying
his blood drowned his guitar. But they
thought it only crying, those who say
that others' death in blood can only count.
No one can die where with green pitch
a playing field courage comes to play
and plucks with ruined stumps   tunes
for us   others   those who need, say
those with cut bodies   violenced
whose braveness makes them share enmity
for others   illimitable   silenced.

15 vii 81

[Untitled]

She was linden, the lime of June,
dark thick the leaves, well grown hair,
under it grows no grass, but hear
how happy run the bees, smell the tune
her graces made. Green scent in quiet air.
I am not light but in the heavy air
hear quiet music brighten the dark lair.

She knows her good. Now remember hate,
the time of driving the hot Interstate:
you cited her, one who'd made pact with love.
Memory before current grace no thing can prove.
She runs, she is quiet, she is exact.
Her quiet music brightens the dark air.

Have you been under the lime,
or seen the way its leaves destroy
all feeble things would grow in leaving time?
But have you also seen the green way
upwards where wings in her scent shine
above the heated roads, those roads where
quiet music may brighten the dark lair?

for Linda Mewshaw   19 vii 81

[Untitled]

In this labyrinth no minotaur sits
Only ranged figures, the other monsters.
As you hand this spool, a strange angel defers
Power to walk in the dark to what occurs
When the double beast assumes it's you he hits.
This spool is the colour of knowing, of silence.

Ariadne, not Mary, chosen to weave the silk
Into the slippery carpets and the rugs,
The true purple, deep like bruises or drugs
Or dreams, runs off the slipping spool and hugs
The dreadful floor, where the monsters look
And watch and wait to see you at the core
The hollow core where the minotaur comes no
    more
And Ariadne goes pale as the palest silk.

This purple silk is coiled on the spool of silence
Cogito ergo sum and that is the sum of defence.
Ariadne's pallor defies the thread she holds
In this dark, this silence, what the labyrinth told
Is worse than the bull beast we knew to be old.
This is new knowledge, what you knew before
Thinks itself off the spool and slithers across the
    floor.
You think you yourself, but must do so in silence
And the silken quiet when monsters have no defence
Against your thinking, your knowing what this is
    for.

On the floor they cast their eyes
In darkness the spool is gone;
Now take it again and walk back into the sun.
The purple, the blackness, the monsters
You may name one by one.

for Bani Shorter   28 vii 81

Self portrait

I'd make myself mad and anxious like Rembrandt
   that you'd know
That the faces of madness are not quite what they
   show.
The straight gaze is the thing you will not allow.

I could make my self and can you ignore how
The painting the self always makes madness grow?
Under the gloss and the tenseness comes now

The straight fact of self no man shall disallow.
You say that speaking the self is banal or low –
I will make myself, the warts, the genius, grow.

None has power now to say my painting is quaint
None to say the verses uncomely, mere paint.
My ugly self shall appal and the soft glaze
Lead you deep to the path and the straight maze.
My mad face stares strict at the viewer come in
   chance;
My portrait asks only my true love to the dance.

                                     4 viii 81

Necessary snobs

Snobbery, thought Carlyle,
Cut hardest in the scared:
Those who have money and
Nothing else, or have talent
And nothing else (certainly no
money). To be a fearful snob
Is an ache waking in a glacial
Morning and not have others' central
Central heating. Snobbery,
Anxiety, jealousy: enemies of love.

But the brave proud snob
Finds ethics and aesthetics one.
Against the rush of bad talk,
Lumping of ill-worn clothes,
Sneer, malice, childish vulgarity:
Reserve, the only guard on values.
Snobbery, pride, respect –
A generous keep of love.

The fine snob's not democratic, but
He wakes still warm under worn rug;
She rises live against easy ugliness.
They are not afraid, they defend
The elegant, the careful, the courteous.
It has nothing to do with money or fear.
Loving what looks right and sounds true
Is preferring the real vulgate of Mozart
To the cult vulgarism of Dylan.

The lyric is our truest snob.
It must be generous to thrive.
But without grace it fails the job,
No snobbism, and it's half alive.
To guard the best's an obligation,
And doing so no scared negation.

5 ix 81

[Untitled]

You knew it then, I know it too
The blood is on the grass like dew

South with North disputes the wealth
that comes from labour or from stealth.
The crafty earning's blatant now,
a mild-faced stumbling sacred cow,
treading the growth, tearing the leaves,
the rich of us, perceived as thieves.

Freedom is for the powerful few
But *blood is on the grass like dew*

The woman and the man debate
Who shall presume to manage hate.
The masks are off: the veils forced on,
Show Salomé's one surviving son.
The face too proud to speak before
Now bodiless must court the poor.
Desire was not for women too
Their *blood is on the grass like dew*

Rebellion spent to little use
Is more than despotism's abuse,
It chokes the flow and stops up strength
And those with power demand at length
Where energy has gone to when
They need it to protect their den.

The rampant rich – domestic men
Are puzzled by the blank drought then.
It seemed so irksome when it poured:
Ignore it, so our power be shored.
But dew shrivels on grass like lime.
All hopeful blood dries up in time.

23 x 81

To account loss

What did we lose?
Accounts must be given.
The terrace of La Coupole, drinking kir,
shopping bags round our feet,
shine of cobbles, the street, our voice.
A father's death remembered
in abrupt white grief, a tower
above us. Your first oyster,
the ice held it, we walked down
the small stables, rain fell through
our ribs. Irresistible impulse to flowers
always, cornflowers and marigolds,
the lily that holds its own tears.
                    (We lost our life
and the right manner to live it)

Speaking words, words always
that were things, that talking was
the best we ever did. And paintings,
I've never seen them since, your knee
constructed the landscape, your eye
gave me bowls of apples, Spaniards
on a balcony, tigers in the wind,
and the tall sharpened man with his child.
                    (We lost our life
and the right manner to live it)

Ah Rome ah Florence ah Paris   places
less of desire than being all I wanted.

In drowning rain at Siena we cabled to friends.
In Modena, tortellini leapt to our mouth.
The bay of silence slid us into ourselves,
books sat half read near the lizards,
we already knew them. (We lost our life
and the right places to have it)

We have now institutions.
We have ambitions.
We own duties. We preserve reputation
in disreputable settings. We list
paintings in reasonable catalogues.
We read texts and note them.
We cook with care and
recognize our parents.
We lost our life, the right places
to live it, and shame
blinds me and starves me
and makes me dumb.
We mislaid life between us
and I can not account for it.

27 x 81

[Untitled]

I take out of my pockets
the past. The strings of loving,
the pressed flowers which bridged time,
always that fatal act to make now
be then. The packets of letters,
the parents marrying picture,
the old property deeds. And, but,
always dialectic I ask how is it
my pockets keep all they lose?

There is a ticket for *Salomé*. There
the engraved paper, some degree
of control. In another corner
see, dusted, the sea urchin
and below the whorled conch.
(Except that you gave it to one
who took it to a meeting, left
the soft pink flare in his office)
The shell is its own sound. Do not,
Do not imagine our space so easy voided.
When we die and go from our place
it stays behind us, echoing not the sea
but pain, mistake, confusion, a sandy
rasping unable to sing or make pearls.
In another fold, the coral teether
chewed by the poet, its bells flat and shrill
as the voices meeting the poet's death by drowning,
his bloated shape held by account of burning,

the well bred cadence shaping the bubbling brain,
the funereal act. The books in our pockets
are wet and stained and sand covers the print.

The veils we saw taken off, the powers
we thought we had earned, the occasions,
the chances, the memorial to love –
they disinter from my pockets, my coat
gets heavier, its damp folds drag my legs.
We are the space our lives remember
nothing well said, it survives as dulled museum,
and the more you turn out returns as the less
of dead speech. These things, these things,
these items of passion and gain are retained
again and again when we do not want them.
In time we empty our pockets
but in space they cannot be voided.
The sharp sounds stop the holes;
gravity claims us to fall in our own past.

31 x 81

Salomé

See her now (temptress?)
Her clothes made by her mother's dressmaker
(an idea of a nubile daughter)
Her unlined feet, clumsy, adolescent.

The court is hot as thought
The courtyard wavy with guards.
She wants the man she thinks of in his pit
To come up and speak, to her.

His words are cant. He serves a man,
and is going to die like his Leader.
She wants in the shade to love him.
He conspires with her stepfather
For a death to appease zealots, or politicians.

She begins to dance. Her mother mistakes
Erotic life as succulent servant of power
(My clever daughter, jiggling her hips –
that's the way to get what we want from him)

But see it's so much simpler.
He wouldn't talk to her, inspired bearded humbug,
so, Give me the prophet's head (She gets it.
Her mother taught her a thing or two)
Now she can play in the cool with his tongue,

Make up conversations. When the talk is overtaken
By punishment soldiers righteously pick off her
   clothes
And sympathize both with the Baptist and Herod.

1 xi 81

[Untitled]

Once I came from silence and lies
And met your gifts – speech and truth.

I walked from emptiness and stony space
And you gave me presence, peopled place.

Then I endured your going and your absence
But this was true – as well – and filled my mouth.

Children were given stones but they were right;
They made noise building your cathedral, your
  light
Monument now their weight on my heart
Gives without knowledge, or true art.

Now I am last proved by your silence.
You'll deny my life and contain your pride.
Against this quiet I've no defence.
You came again – cast silent teeth wide
And I see dragons spring up from mute man –
This apprehension, this farming, what woman can
Construct devouring or – be quiet to scan
The stony path down which his terror ran?

I am no woman so my lie grows
On you your beauty your truth shows.

6–7 xii 81

[Untitled]

Let others be the grammar of the world
You said, but what if there was no world
Only the syntax of passage to
An imagined city, imaginary clauses
To dependent rooms which each held
Only ideas of journey, and death?
There is a high wall to one side
It says completeness as the knuckles
Graze, eyes turn the curve,
But because a circle, it's never
Finished.
           There are doors
Opening, to other doors,
Drafts through solid masonry.
We meet those we run from
Coming against us; the black dog
Leads us, knows their leash
Of hounds, takes avoiding paws
Down streets leading from the city.
There is an enduring curfew
The birds stop speaking at dusk
Gates close but we scale them
And find we are inside, again.
Gashed pigs thrown with leaves
Lie in the gutters which run.

Now comes the poet, not signing releases,
Nor saying we have pastoral places,

Neither commissioning any pauses,
Only allowing partitive clauses –
Of the birds silent at dusk
Of the hounds tracking nowhere
Of unlucky blood in the gutters
She is quiet. She says grammar
Will be our hypothesis,
Now sings that other parts of speech
Do not exist except to breech
The walls we must think may complete
That last and needed messy street
To show up syntax as pretence
And curve a world to last silence.

8–10 xii 81

[Untitled]

There is this thing of dying out of spite:
The time was wrong, the publisher corrupt;
They wouldn't listen so let's prove us right
By making up hearers who can't interrupt.
Maybe the syntax is not quite the form
To shout about how urgent was our need
To disallow the normal and show harm
Where others saw a kind of normal feed.
We were taught novel courses and at last rebelled:
The prose was decent and distinctly moral
But a more frantic need could not be quelled,
The fat desire to get us crowned in laurel.
We killed ourselves, we died, we scarcely heard
Voices determining how we owned the word.

4 ii 82

[Untitled]

When I hurt most then must I least resent
For all this time I've guarded my own place
But no mistaking that the cuts were meant
And you have left me, merely, blood-stained space.
You urgent call me and demand support
But when it's offered thrust the thing away.
As if you thought loving were some sport
Or all the talk only a kind of play.
You say resenting is what makes me up:
Consider, that you've never counted cost,
Thought you could cut and thrust, then merely
    stop,
Violence so casual it saw nothing lost.
My hard resentment came from pricing high
Things which might hurt me, but which you let lie.

30 i 82

[Untitled]

Histories of love are not uncommon
Only its buildings rare.
See that dome make its own collapse –
Two kinds of demolitions: one by firing –
The small inserted tubes design implosion
Show eloquent space can be exactly cancelled
– the other, neglect, to rain and sand, to rubble.

If I should write you how I once had loved you
You would deny the force of my hypothesis.
If I had loved you as I now can write you
You will correct the grammar of my strength.
You are yourself in the tired passages
You excel in leaping walls.
There, you accomplish your demolition.
The extraordinary marble, the gold, the roof
Shattered to bits, mosaic, sharded colours.

Into this desert I come with notebook
And write down pieces which cut as I handle.
Building, this building, thinking its shape exhausts
    me,
I draft centuries, late or crossed addition
Finer than the first shape now one sees better.
O golden golden heart such structure for
    destruction.

Let us imagine, now: This dome rises
Columns and arches give shade, there is a garden.

Mosaic runs up around each separate twisted pillar.
There is water, there are children, paintings.
We dig the trenches, and dust, and label
And slow out of the bits a face begins.
This Pantocrator judges but defies the Judgement
His hand accretes and leads Adam from Hell
Abortive sands yield up imagination
Give up the shape which made a hand that built.

I rot with heat and dust and the notebook
Blots. But from this ruin I have remade
The great building. On this plain, in the sun,
For miles and miles watched over by the guns
The great face emerges, our judge
Our beauty, the face, our past, the grand design.
(You may disdain me as I sketch this for you
Sometime tomorrow others will come and bomb it
Moreover notebooks may be lost or stolen
But can you say remaking wasn't worth it?)

They built as they could, so also we.
And then collapses, and then those like me.
I excavate intentions, hypothesise the motives,
By a slow, dusty, accretion re-invent
The fabulous palace or dome
That should exist.

14–18 i 82

[Untitled]

Further to this say why it must be done:
Vallejo, Tsvetayeva, your poems of lost republics
Writing collapse of freedom's never fun.

It must be done because last year's panic
Makes the flight of the fox and hanging in exile
To run be dead to speak and then be sick

Not enough for meaning not just enough
Not even a bit to make the troops smile
Nor yet the amount to make free bodies
Write us the right stone – *I had this
from Marina, these beads*, on that train –
And from Montrouge came those remains
Their widow wrote (another translating the while)
they'd wept *for her, Georgette* –
Do corpses strain? Does their neck break the earth?
Or revolutions done in the music hall of war?
The fox is running still and the long drop's far.

Widows take us up. Lovers resume us
Only because the panic seemed important
Somebody thought the pain worth some fuss.
The film, that dance re-live the death of poets
It doesn't matter, except for those like us –

Spain or Russia (in fact, Paris or exile)
Allow republic to be made from waste

Only if some can listen, or watch and not smile
At wasted lives, those like foxes running
Passed and over the river, taught dogs cry the time.
It's deep, breath's messy, informal cries call out
From deep valleys they who know the kind
Those who attempt free state,
Whose ear is all half lost, want that shout.

They press on the earth hard
Their feet disrupt the plain
But we thought they'd come
For cry of loss of freedom
For hearing a tongue thrown over a cliff
For knowing an ear wasted to the trite
(to assure some safety to
make sure it wasn't performance)
For seeing spoilt life's nothing
So long as their fox can bite.

25 i 82

[Gay Clifford's notes on the preceding poem]

César Vallejo (1892–1938), Peruvian, author of *España aparta de mí esta caliz*. Based in Paris from 1923 to his death. A Marxist, visited Russia, wrote *Rusia en 1931*; visited Spain and associated with writers of the Left. Was ordered from France by the police, again returned to Spain, and during his absence the police sacked his apartment. Died of undiagnosed illness – 'acute intestinal infection' – the day the Fascist offensive reached the Mediterranean. Buried in Montrouge, the 'Communist' cemetery. Georgette Vallejo, his widow, had his body moved to Montparnasse in the sixties. The gravestone reads 'J'ai tant neigé/pour que tu dormes/Georgette.'

Marina Tsvetayeva (1894–1941), Russian, author of *Verses about Moscow*, *Poems for Akhmatova*, *Poems for Blok*, *Poem of the End*. A life of persistent poverty: during the Moscow famine put her younger daughter into a State orphanage where the child died of hunger. Friend of Pasternak, Blok, Mandelstam, Akhmatova and Rilke. Went into exile in 1922 in Prague, Paris and elsewhere. Returned to Moscow in 1939: her daughter was arrested two months later, her son three. Evacuated to Yelabuga when war came, where she hanged herself in 1941. Two months later Akhmatova was on a train and someone noticed the beads she was wearing; she said, 'That was a present from Marina.'

[Untitled]

This alliance came in dark from stark plea
In movement, the taxi cutting across the city.
It yields three presents: the clock, the fish, the book.
– and then the greatest, our own romantic
    language –
That shall keep time, that other dash through silver,
The last restore knowledge of others' weakness.
Frailty, your name is male; and I allied
With all you brought to get the greatest gift –
A mouth for passion only to make time, keep
    course,
Print straight and last to move to speech.

In blackness I claimed you and you now move well:
Keep your own time: but don't resent the pillage
I make your text and tongue – deliver
My grave maker, the timed and measured space;
To this favour you must come.
This river you must swim.
This clock stops, this fish dies, this book blurs.
Only my language stops the death or blurring
And this you must ally with in your turn.
The gauntlet's down: reseize your things,
There's no forgiving, hell and no, there's not.

But yes, grace in time of movement,
The book as record, the new speech,

We have to listen. Gulls displaced from the sea
Scream over dark mornings so our ear can be
Forced to attention, catch where we went from.
We came from water, we time our own migrations,
Those we love most print out the greatest damage
Yet leave us speech; re-done, undone, again.

The clock, the fish, the book, and then the talking.
We leap obstacles, merge in high waters,
Then down the barriers in time comes our child.
It can't tell time, ignores swimming,
Can't cope with books but if we listen
It speaks. We must abandon
The gifts of definition and assume the risk
To speak, to speak; those lips I hung on
(only at last a grin of bone and death)
Are made to flow rivers, to show light bodies
Fled from their space, breaking the face of time,
Being at once together in their tongues.

Come out of blackness, cross a city,
Dismiss your gifts as symbols, take time.
Read the pages that swim from darkness,
Do not imagine speaking is a crime.
Our history's made by the surprised hand,
The startled mouth that found that it could say
All sorts of love, and then give them away.
Hands bring presents, stretch for an opposite land
But as they drop them, are worth what they say.
It shall be re-invented, our strident way of alliance;
We make our transport, our speech is our best hand.
The gulls fly off, salmon jump, Alexandria burns,
Poets can front the time as we shall learn.

22 i 82

The Fable of the Dragon and the Princess

Someone observed that 'Dragons aren't discreet' –
Only last week I met one in the street:
She mopped her eyes and scales, and softly said:
You won't believe what that St George just did –
There was I, quietly chatting to my friend
(Andromeda, a girl to whom I send
Postcards and things; I think she's lonely –
She *will* live on that cliff, which isn't only
Hard and uncomfortable, but also chilly,
Some of her family think she's simply silly).
Anyway, there I was, we talked away
And I'd ignited a nice bale of hay
To keep her warm, and brew a pot of tea –
She seemed most pleased to have a call from me.
Suddenly, up came George, in shining armour;
He clearly was in right boy-scout ill-humour.
He clashed around and made a fearful din,
Muttering lots of things about the sin
Of dragons who aspire to talk to girls
Who should be tending to their pretty curls
(It's true we were discussing Latin
But that's more gripping than the price of satin).
His horse looked rather tired under the weight
Of all that hardware and fine moral freight
Of declamation (he'd sooner go away,
Forget St George, and munch at some fresh hay).
Our hero dashed towards us, drew his sword,
I was so scared I couldn't say a word.

He waved his weapon, and cried out *Avaunt!*
Beware all dragons who princesses daunt.
This wasn't quite the point, as you'll agree –
We were there sharing friendly cups of tea.
I then remembered I could spout out flame
And did so: but young George came on the same.
I twitched my tail (I fear I even growled),
Andromeda seemed bored, and when he howled
Said: O, these knights are tedious!
They always come at tea-time, say they need us
To be delivered by their mighty strength
In order to be made a Saint at length.
He cut my tail a bit, but nothing bad,
Save that the awful thing, what's really sad,
Is that he took Andromeda to live with him
And when I 'phoned her she was using Vim
To shine his armour: he'd a new assignation
Saving some other girl of noble station.

The dragon paused and said: I shouldn't say
How much this scene distressed me; but, I pray,
Do please consider, dragons can be discreet
They aren't the ones who challenge knights they
    meet –
Is it perhaps that stories make us be
The frightful creatures other people see?

                                    3 ii 82

141

And such a wall as I would have you think, that had in it, a cranny'd hole or chink

My crannyed hole – through which I came
Gave me life, but reticent the same,
Allowed me time to speak my life.
After the tiredness came disappointment:
Daughter no salve, nor ointment nor good wife.
This you accounted for, held up your hand
And between fining fingers showed space
Where those who'd hated might now retrace
Their parents' ill into another place.
A place of death – if misunderstood,
The scarf bloodied, and caused wounds
At last made to utter sounds
That out of tragic action would make
Delight, what we take
In seeing that the desperate bloodied start
Can be resumed by unassuming art
Into the silly actor's part.

This for my mother who made more than she knew
But had the wit to know what she might do
With the preposterous bloody thing she had
Hung to her life. She picked up the scarf,
Chased off the lion, made the audience laugh
And made the tragic comic and not sad.

Who can imagine walls aren't penetrated?
They're only solid while we hated;
But then comes up the love to breach space
And make us laugh each other into place.

2 iii 82

Body politic

What body's politic? Its needs, its greeds,
Fearful urge to handle well and be handled
To run democracy right, to sow seeds
That might bring up dragons, be muddled
To weeds. Taking risks the body is about
And when I shout I do that words shall out
And say the body's the best thing we have.
To do other were cowardice. Only in bodies
Democracy lives; only there does true shape give
Amelioration to the common urge or force
To push us from things we think; of course,
Coarse and dull and facile; but now think –
Through every cell runs a power to shrink,
Small it may be. But gold
Was always in small things
Sold to be about the body.

Love us now, do not forget the atom,
Sudden pulse, rage or need for quiet,
The calm covers laid over sleep,
The hand that hands us linen while we weep.

My sweet friend and other body
I need you; do you have courage
To say as I do?
I will deliver you but by no murder;
I am that one whose hearing's harder –
I cast off Judith; she boasted how

She'd killed the man while not allowing
How she'd played with him. I will not
Do that. Do you have courage
To say in bodies may be made true marriage?
Say as I do – there's nothing else
But corporal truth. That Blake knew.
So do I.
Can you give me some other reason why?

8 iii 82

If you are the Colonel's daughter

If you are the Colonel's daughter
But a radical to boot
You're supposed to hate his métier
Don't give a hoot.

If you are the son of a dead Jew
But a scholar as well
They'll say you must be Zionist too
Tell them go to hell.

If your mother was a housewife
And you a feminist
You'll be meant to think she lost her life
You may think what you missed.

Your father came from a Southern state
You were an alien bred
You're supposed to inherit its hate,
Not your own political bed.

We're presumed to be our origins —
Or, betray ourself.
Why not let both sets of sins
Make another wealth?

Not to take easy ways-out
That's the thing.
To know when to strike and when to shout
And to sing.

Resist the generations false ideologies
Be clear and present and past:
Learn not to please.
Know what you had of parents' identities,
Also learn to cast
Net of them and weapons you seize
For dual power to last.

20 iii 82

The blood-letters: Pilate?
Lady Macbeth?

It's felt that cutting others up was possessive
It's thought their letting of blood aggressive:
What about those notes
We wrote at school,
Cutting our fingers with pencil sharpening tool?

They weren't true blood-letters: but political sense
Gave them meaning themselves too dense
To have. They killed the odd man;
Ambitious people go for what they want;
What of the writers who cut as they scan?

Blood-letters, that's what poets are
Taking every meaning steps and cuts too far,
Writers cut their hand
To scrawl love-letters or rage,
Find the page husbands or friends cut by demand.

Worlds make war now without letting blood.
If you want power you can cinder people and
    should
Preserve property, not messing the street,
Go in to clean towns only sweep some dust:
Sensual word sense knows lovers' veins bleed the
    sheet.
Writers' dread blood letters see the heads cut.
Mandelstam, Tsvetayeva, even Keats,
The birds falling wingless, the ice cracked,

Teutonic Knights cut blood, ignorant.
Words' knowledge more awful because sapient.
To be not blood-letter – but to let blood
And blood flows and all true letters be
Bloody true hurtful but what passion meant.

1 iv 82

For an American novelist
and scholar

I entered the wood late, too late,
Not middle of the road but middle age.
Found neither wolves nor dusk
Only in harsh light the fish in trees
And hateful birds slithering under leaves.

My gestures shall haunt you as I go this light,
You shall not have satisfaction doing right.
As Absolom hung by Isadora hair
I shall now hang whenever you go there.
In this bright wood the scarf of words
Shall fall and haunt. You'll choke
And grasp Company swords.

Wolves dig under snow that aerial hunters
Can't kill. Your technics now has made
Both in the wood and its margins – those not afraid.
Still we will come no sainted Beatrice
And hang in hot light and brush your face
With every dumb and violent thing you made.

See, fish within, wolves beyond, and the bright
    wood.
This path you could have written if you would.

5 iv 82

Timor mortis conturbat me

I that in hell was, and gladness
Flesh is brittle and the Fiend sly.
But on that fear and brittleness
Love shall arrange a supple corpse
To be laid out and, may be, better talk.

'She was a real bitch' (a last-word Annie)
But as we view her, still – we can't complain
Some amount of verbal fanny
But still resisting *timor mortis*
Did not confound, she fought. And spoke
Timor mortis non conturbat me.

My father, my maker, when you go
I'll have a wake that shall show
Your excellence. As your women pace
All space you gave us
No fear in that place

20 iv 82

[Untitled]

She is – yellow as primrose or gorse
And most handsome in her mother's tracksuit
Which is also yellow (if a bit large to the foot)
But above it all she carries clear eyes and a nose
Which can snoot into the future & not be opposed.

She has made a present to me
And she's first to benefit.
These golden bindings came from her
And on her desk they'll sit.

You see, dear Kate, a present made
Is better than one bought
From this brilliant yellow shade
We can share sun and thought.

The daffodils will not run, away, soon –
You will have marigolds in your light of noon.
The primrose glistens damp & is yellow and pales
But in your time when courage fails
Gold roses inspire your room.

You early caught a lesson it takes others years to
    know
The presents we make allow us to take all the love
    we show.

                                        22 iv 82

Ended Causes

And there remaining nothing further to be done in this cause, it is ordered that *this matter is stricken from the docket and the papers placed among the ended causes.*

> Slingsby J. Marshall, Clerk, Circuit Court for the County of Albemarle, Commonwealth of Virginia

This matter is stricken,
Or again, even rotten.
Nice to have it recognized
An ended cause, if not wise.
The papers, they're the thing –
Who will at last play the string?
One who took trouble to write
The way others would misuse power –
Even a penguin can be skinned white.

But again and again, I say do
Do not rejoice – my hard
Iambic shall string your heart,
You played art but lost that left
There's none left, now, but not by their part.

Even a penguin can be skinned white
By any with training enough to catch
A flapping thing with its odd voice.
This matter is indeed stricken
It was not a matter for choice.

Among ended causes I'd cite
Futile writing of what we might
Have made ourselves. But when penguins
Are caught and skinned, and eaten
The wolves arrive and are not beaten.

Stricken from dockets, the young and fierce survive
They are the ones who should be still alive.

20 v 82

The cellars of Sidon

Tyre is down
Hundreds lie dead in the cellars of Sidon
Cities my cities and your ruins
Rubble and walls, but carbonized bodies;
Stones replaced but never veins.
Jesse broken, his prophetic tree
Scorched dry as vines near Pompeii.
Hundreds dead in the cellars of Sidon.

And other cities where the dead don't rot
For fine nice weaponry we now have got.
Dust in the streets which can be easy swept,
Bricks seen again, not those who birthing wept
Shadows on walls and Dresden bombed to hell
Through smoke a question: did we do this well?
Like porcelain bits the bones say what is gone
Dead in the cellars of Sidon.

Cities your cities, they are ruined dead,
Yet what is that beside a shattered head?
What of obstetrics which made war from labour
And conned the workers to our children's murder?
We say Dark Ages but how dark are these
When swollen piles of calcined bodies freeze?
Limepit waited carts of Plague or the Black Death
Our clean arms salesmen bank on others' breath.
Remember when the city's gone
What's in the cellars of Sidon.

The ochre walls, the gentle terraces
The cafés towers mosques and whore-houses
Apses, arcades and beams, worn clothes drying in
    air,
Leisurely eating, child's voice, alleys and shops and
    hair,
The plants in tins, roses and bergamot.
The laughing fucking walking speaking lot.
When we extinguish this and when they're gone
Think on Tyre *and the cellars of Sidon.*

20 vi 82

Money as good a weapon
as the gun

I don't want an orderly funeral
Nor be good enough to be dead,
With Katyn wood (or the pits of hell)
Who'd imagine to do that well?
Marriage, that hot and bitter South,
The houses, porches dropping, mouth,
The ageing face, plants in dry dirt
And impotence masculine unsaid hurt.

I believe in Hell. It's a handy male notion.
But their punishment grows me a heavier motion
Down, on and on, I see gaolers dumb,
They are the ones who make writing come.

South the vines rot & all blacks have got
Is much the same as the Arab lot.
Rot in cellars, on porches, or in bright sun
Money as good a weapon as the gun.

6 vii 82

Autumn

It is not summer makes our hopes or fears
But is its death that shuffles feet and rears
The way we have to hack and dig and prune again

We have to hack and dig and prune the plain
The plant retires and bares the clammy pain
It is not summer shows our hopes or fears

No well bred summer parents hopes and fears
The roses rot, the crops are soaked with rain
Only the wind bares teeth to try again

The bared teeth and the tangled hair again
Throw off the roses, vines, and apples too
The summer dead leaves us a toughened few

The summer's dead leave us the toughest few
No grapes, no vintage, no consoling fruit
Only good ill wind chilling face and foot

This fierce wind chilling our working head and foot
But still we run over the crumbling plain
The sweet praised crops go, and display the strain

Jarred up, by others, crops embalm the strain
Yet we the toughest run a wind stripped land
Over half-covered piles of dead who can't demand.

That harvest dead some gloat. We must demand
Cold naked judging heat under a sun to stare
It's not our summer made the hope. The fear.

22 ix 82–11 x 82
Beirut

For Connie Fields and the
women riveters

'In '41 they couldn't wait to get us to work
But riveting that's something. Y'see
That time the ship is trusted and worth
The water is making a thing.' '45, '46
The tune changed: 'It was a whole
Different tack – make babies to free
A nation from those dead men.' Mean, that
Whole different tacky use of power.
I am the riveter, I outfaced the officer
Who'd learnt boot-camp kicking blacks should
    prosper
That strange America liberty built from fear.

And, in another country, my parents marry.
It is 1937 and he is in his dress blues,
One medal. 24, what did he do for it?
(Carried the colour at the Coronation)
My mother's mouth confident, I suppose
She has done the right thing, yet in her eyes
(Spectacles since two, they'd told her brides don't
    wear them)
A blurred look, like doubt. He wears his blues,
His spurs, and his hands, taught
By the drill sergeant rest light on his sword.
And his mouth under incipient moustache, seems
    caught.
His eyes are brilliant: they can't look to each other.
Her startled roses and his still braid make one afraid.

From sleek chest to a Peter Pan collar
From shined Wellingtons to her hidden feet
From the men who let you make a war dollar
To the woman who slogged, and then had the fleet
Take her out of her job. Well; no speech.

Yet historians find riveter's power.
That *beautiful ship – to have made something*
Is something. Or the taxing child.
Haunted our age as we looked
Possibly a first time to each other.
Politics, yes. Money, yes. Domestic well
Who's to be free? In catastrophic mild
Conventional cutting our freedom comes,
The voice that's radical, chartist, and thumbs
Up the medal, lost job, crumbled dress. Liberty's
    hooked
On those who lost it as the flame joined steel
Or understanding (Harris, Photographers,
    Chatham)
We were in chains and still could make out free.

They don't nomore need plated ships and the Mess
    silver
(Tureens, four; Marrow spoons, 3 dozen; six troph-
    ies; 12 doz. soup spn)
Were auctioned out at Chatham, if some valued
Artifice to serve power. What of artificers'
Skill, detailed and rough, who took convention
And made subversion free the unknowing child
    from weapons?

Intelligent hands on swords concur
The woman's voice on the waterfront
'I'd like us to do the same
Again, but not for war.'

4 xii 82

Marvell's and the Archbishop's Turtle

Archbishop Laud, savant and man
Who loved most things that crawl and can
Instruct us that we knew, or show
No antiquarian womb is slow,
Placed in his Lambeth Palace grounds
A tortoise – 1628 – whose bounds
Were leisurely. The learned came
And viewed that curious unwilled tame
Slow-stepping carapace. Inside
His nature hated cold. He died.
In 1754. The gardener dug
Him rashly out from leaves, his rug.
Perhaps from Africa or Spain
Our winters forced evading pain.

In Italy, I saw him there
Stubbed learned feet pointing to earth
His snout and shell muzzled with juice.
We called him Churchy for the femme
And sent him loose to let him home.

They do not plod
But Tuscans hate
The ancient and deliberate.
The road was hot and he not sharp.
Smashed by a hot and casual axe
The green four-quartering shell and snout
Wrinkled as ants winkled him out.

Loathe a cold war and see the freeze
As northern fantasies disease.
But the Archbishop had he lived
To see his tortoise rudely digged
Into a frost in which his shell
Became a dead still icicle
Then might have argued, or have not.
Yet loved the oldest thing he'd got.

Hating the cold, liking his plot
Archaic sanity wants heat.
His squared-up smile made him to treat
The old lives should possess some heat.

9 xii 82

Donne and Pope, St Lucie's being the longest night of the year

No half placed verses but a prose run mad
And had yours done so then you might have had
Remembered things you had and then gone bad.
The shortest day all you could give for loot
Remember her, remember her, who the bed's foot
Gave then some life; but could not make your wife,
Remember me, now as light shrinks your life.
My eyes can't shine on plate or Christmas tree
And this not wise but what is seen shall be
All lovers' alchemy to shine, to see
The mere iconographic sight you had me be.
Eyeless, prosaic, this mad world I see
Now is the longest night. I am not cast
To see that blackness isn't wisdom's waste
And now no verse. St Lucie's eyes on plate
See back the coming through some poets' hate,
And this long night an alchemy we wait.
The hour a vigil, and eve shall renew
A seeing sharp should then have been quite due.
This is life's midnight, but gazing sharp
Better than bearing the outdated harp.

22 xii 82

Epitaph for a standing army

They went, and thought no sky suspended.
They fought, finely; and then some terrain ours.
A Government imagined it had ended
Battles done well before the count of hours.

They did quite right; seventy miles well –
But as a burned face or widow gets a cross
As parade dress becomes voting capital
Think we could somehow not have had such loss.

They are piped out. Such a bloody waste
So far to go to be sunk. I trust
Those who chose to do this, to do it well;
And when they can not then we shall face hell.
No fight without order. No taking monied haste.
Damn politicians. Save those who are lost.

29 xii 82

Demise of a middle class

Some things must be done; you'll go mad at last
And write off others' history, but without haste.
When you have taken from trunks medals and
    swords and guns,
Off the banisters a bear's pelt your grandfather
    shot
Then found it a mother and had to kill the lot,
The pelisse with scarlet ruching, the lead model
    cruiser,
Letters nested by mice, case of fruit knives
Mother of pearl impact in velvet, that accumula-
    tion of lives;

When you find out one who lost family courage
    and runs,
When known all their taste and courage and fear,
    your words
Shall perhaps give you the freedom.
But of what city? Is it large? Is its sky blue?
When cash runs out how do you get there too?
Do not retain too much, though you had to do.
Consider your own land, touch what they were
    but last
We are all mercenaries in face of historical fact.
When you start the bonfires to send this up in
    flames,
No loss of nerve, remember particular names.

This careful terrain, its rocks its waterfalls,
Drawing rooms, box trees were built for you
In a sense. Yours to pick over the relics
And be dangerous to know, if you know what calls.

3 i 82

For W.E. [William Empson]

He was great perhaps the best and there was sun
Jungled grass and blood peonies dispensed what
    was gone
She asked him the cat's name and he said – *Cat, of*
    course.
His disregard for names possibly made things
    worse.
Later in cold indoors his camel dressing gown
The impeccable voice and the spare frame
Were quiet over space and his own fame
Not easy think and be constant to one who's great
Simpler to sneer or hate and be extant.
But up his standing and his strong reply.

Tired and bored because better than most
Winter gardens evade most frost
Orange cat and green jungle and the poet great
Lucky to have had these and survival instead of
    hate.

12 i 83

For Dottie and E. P. Thompson

I observe I exhibit the same fearful compulsion
To make others' writing machines work at the dead
    of night.
Is the night quite dead? you may ask and my God
    think
What a world would be like without the noise of
    dolphins
Playing quietly and in a mood ready always to listen
To the cries for help from a hundred miles off.
Think of a world without the squeal of otters
Or the fat greedy cry of grebes; we must not do it.

Now I deliver to my friends
Their writing exploited to own ends.
The cry of dolphins chirruping
Noise of the otter, larking
And the stupid dog who went down
And could not get up without
Frail two-legs of some age to help
Him up the cliff of memorial concrete
To make sure he'd dry without a world's yelp.

My friends, we are dying and not for we're malign
The Russians use rhetoric and not how we align,
If I give you dolphins, if I deliver you otters
Think how this bloody age has made us history's
    squatters.
I hope in a far sea a dolphin shall take this from us,

Gulls and otters still speak language of promise;
There is not much that we dare hope or praise
Except having a future to raise.

In the day the dolphins cry
Otters do delight the eye
Faint, under water, slow, sympathy comes
Not all friends think these are the drums.
In the day the dolphins cry
Otters do delight the eye.
This our black night, so make it go
And live with light where dolphins show.
In the day the creatures cry
And flesh and fish delight the eye.

29/30 i 83

[Untitled]

Poetry burns. O yes believe it
As wrinkled and wet we come from the great flood
When we have to look at the last dog in the Prado
As the days of death get worse and the damson
    sickens
Then listen. There are voices in these hands
Let them be held over you as bedraggled from
    history
You need fire from those who have paid a price.
It is the first fire and it is honest
It is fire of love and rage and help
It is fire that shall not burn trees
Or hate those jostled into starvation
At a second's notice. Fire to release
From damp and terrible accident some clay
Of observation. We have eaten our wars in our
    hearts
And the price is paid in our terrible love
Not perhaps love domestic, nor perhaps
Decorous. But we are the paediatricians of language,
The rubber gloves of words give you your fiery
    future.
Not much my friends, but there are fires worse.

There are no free men left to praise
Nor many free women at the start
These hot hands are obliged to raise
Fuel from the damson's heart.

Not destroying, only making the days
Shine with the fire of the heart.

As the *auto da fé* goes on
As the grass is withered and gone
See this un-envious burning and take
What perhaps to their cost poets make.

5 ii 83

Was your great-uncle Ezra Pound?

He'd always been a–political.
Even at Eton, already a brilliant linguist,
He got away with extra French (no gentleman
can be thought a swot) by pretending
They were reading pornographic novels.
Clever old K. they said. He was less
And more smart than they knew.

Some decades later, proficient in seven languages,
A safe man, his diplomatic career stopped.
He fell in love with a widow who
admired Mussolini. Temporarily boggled
by love, he was caught by a British photographer
with his hand in the Fascist salute.
Telegrams from London. Old K. out.
The rest of his life was Rome, not Venice.
Luckily, Italians forgive. *Eccellènza*
They'd say in the local shops, have a seat.
Can we cash your cheque? My boy
will deliver the goods. Fortune caught him.
His step-son, by then a light of the Fascists,
threw him out of his flat for reasons of greed.
The step-grandchildren, warm from beating–up
Socialists in Piazza del Popolo
Rifled his boxes. He moved to a flat
Near the pyramid of Cestius. Keats is there.
By that stage he wouldn't have cared.

Booted into a cage at 83. Pound let from his
When 73. I have a friend, a great painter
It happens, who went so mad in the war
They shipped him home to the States in a cage.

If you get to be that old, if you have to
Choke your mistakes, does it matter whether
You acted from belief or love?
Error, error, always stupid error.
He didn't know the world believed other things.
Pound believed the Jews were the cause of
Usura. Even Zola in *Money* was not dumb for
That mistake. When I took a Jew to the pyramid
He wept at Keats' grave. Too young to know
How odd or dangerous politics may be.

Dangerous because random. Random in dangers
Making enemies friends, and families strangers,
Making poets stupid when we need them to be
    bright,
Blotting out intelligence and humane light.
I have now a mirror, on the back E.K., K.S.
A King's scholar from Eton, and into that mess:
On the shelves *The Cantos*, in a good edition
And Mussolini's photograph to show no remission.

We hang things upside down.
When I saw Pound lunching at Raffaelle's
He was feeding bread to the birds, not
Looking at them. Later he'd play chess
With a friend who sculpted, for Washington
Cathedral even. Last of my great-uncle
Was a fine frail body sitting inside good tweed,
And not looking at paintings, though I saw
When I turned down his bed, he was still
Reading Chekhov in Russian. I've always
Voted Socialist, and know why so.

Yet these old men went wrong, and blame
I can't do.

We hang things upside down, not always villains.
Things get caged, and we get smug, just to show
   willing.
Little knowledge as great fault as too much.
I know of Cobalt 60 and of Agent Orange
But know belief and learning are as fallible traps
As ignorance or nonchalance, and having to take the
   rap.

                                             7 iii 83

Parasitic poem

She was told her estate was bankrupt
And nothing to possess.
She thought spoils from Poynton and kept
The horse, just to go to that mess.

It was cold, bloody cold, like New York winters,
Icicles covered every pane with the splinters.
A fire in the study: she burned the odd book.
Then not loosing her coat went to take a look.

In the ball-room frescoes by Luca Signorelli
Dead returned and writhed; the retiring-room
    stank.
The kitchens commodious but somehow dank.
It was the bedrooms seemed sinister smelly.

Four Rubens, a Greuze (unappetizing), a fat sleek
    great Stubbs.
Needless to say in her Father's room, above golf
    clubs.
Every night his white tie tied under that horse;
He probably never saw it, what's worse.

She walked down the old, beautiful, Turkey rug.
The old man was impatient, the Gentileschis waited,
Assigned to the gun-room. Women were hated.
She put on her hat and left what seemed smug.

He painted in the garden. Young and quite dark.
She noted his painting. Gwen John? quite a lark.
Then abruptly she thought, not live out this sham,
I've now no estate and I don't give a damn.
His jacket and her hat got wet: they punted
On all the disreputable that had to be shunted.
Shaking with laughter, they watched up the flames.
And she knew who did it; but did not give names.

One painting she dragged out the library window:
A small girl, her sister, a new-born brother akimbo.
Green silks, ten inches. The painter spoke:
If I'd made that you'd never have been broke.

Small things can move us more than our estate.
It's what we carry singed can make real debate.

15 iv 83

The Turkish Bowl

Unlike the golden bowl
This is unbroken
It has eaten its own fissures
Aligned its own fractures.
It is not love
It is for holding it
Self and the breaks of self.
The leaves flower in, to sapphire and purple
The base flares straight to white buds.
You calix, stamen, design
Held unknown substance
Yet kept and held
The cracks to become celestial
All we should be if globes were just.
Ovals of daisies, forget-me-not, amaranthus
We hand to the other in silence
Loving breakable things.
Put in it fishes or tears
Your enemy's hot dead heart, the honey
Hate and debate of mad power.

The bowl can be washed and is there
And amaranth, melancholy, daisy. Complete
the pure fact. We can not possess.

14 iv 84

Happiness

Delight is in doing
And doing means learning facts.
And what's a fact? It is happiness
Knowing the real exists.
It does not have a limbo, an inferno
There there are no un-baptized
Spinning the void, and no Francesca da Rimini
Spinning the void, or man who knew her fear.
Nel gran diserto – how great a desert.

This wilderness the happy cross at a loss
For they go to the happiest mountain.
It has small sharp sweet herbs at its side
It's the start and reason of all happiness.
They sing going up the delectable slope
Theirs their mistress and their author
I took from her the style has done me honour.
It includes the man in the rush-hour
Carrying delphiniums at Victoria.
The small pots of sweet peas under
Photographs. The very carefully laid
Trays for breakfast. The annoying
Blackbird who shrieks and chitters at dawn.
Delightful cleaned and shimmering silver.
The sharp edge of the well ironed linen.

I love abstraction and even distraction
But to be called to the mountain of fact

Is to have under your feet the song of things
Being. The song of the hump-backed whale.
So enter then her gates with praise,
Approach with joy her courts unto;
The happiest thing is to know that
A fact is greater than its definition.
Whales. Linen. Hills. Flowers. Women.
Why else should we use a phrase like
Having a lark.?

10 vii 84

A hand at dominoes

2 fives, 2 fours, 3 sixes, 2 threes, 1 four

Five things conspired:
Fate, fertility, father, friend and mother, fortune.
The five continued to the second face,
And in a third reduced to four.
The dread number. (In her mind, pink and edgy)
Boarding school. No father.
Same again at fourth.
But then a six; Gods for a good throw!
A double six: the Oxford First.
Another six. The jobs, so sweet.
She had drawn the male world as her own.
But on the eighth face it comes down:
Nothing but green three, envy, emulation, ending.
Back down on the ninth three; energy, agony; and
        nothing.
There is a failed marriage somewhere.
Now the dominoes come to the tenth.
(The *outcome* in the Tarot)

Four, square.
Blue, colour of hope and faith.
She construes her fortune –
Perhaps?

	Learning	Love
	Loss	Living
Or?		
	Mother	Father
	Despair	Daughter

She takes off her domino
Goes to the party as herself
She is *en travestie*
But no Proust,
Thanks to the fates
Drew her such a hand.

15 xi 84

Journalist retrieves poem
from tape

Why did she love him?
Because she never proved him.
He wrote well, elegantly,
Used table-napkins reluctantly,
Laughed buoyantly and gently.
He could weep over poems
Lowell, or Raleigh, or Blake.
Also enjoyed puns. He
Had beauty and energy to
Make any heart ache.

He repaired her bicycle
He had a charming alert dog
Battersea waif or strayer,
He laughed in his sleep,
Washed up meticulously and not
Officiously.
Above all things he was always fun.
Intelligent, instructive,
That makes for some ways
The hearts sing.
Better to know
Than prove.

24 x 84

From the south; to my father

Father, my father? Where are you?
(How often theology has printed out that cry)
You have supported.
Changed fuses. Tolerated ruses.
But where are you?

When I see you, so small
Straight and elegant, like a Birmingham greyhound
My heart leaps to my mouth.
I imagine a person with vast waste inside.
Where the wind howls and polar bears
Come and crack your innards for
A bully's treat. (As they did, at your school)
I get up and dress and go out. And wind tears
Scarf from my shoulders and my fears.
(I'm become like something from *Alexandr Nevsky*)

My boots get lost in the mud.
Where you are is cold.
I must warm you, must take you
Somewhere where people giggle and jostle and
    sweat.

But no, you still run, are there;
There where only the foxes scuffle beneath
Snow. And the Trans-Siberian rail
Can not catch you.
How much less, your daughter.

My dress freezes stiff on my bones
I am now a Wykeham-Fiennes
It is so cold inside you.
I want to light a great fire.
Running still, I wonder if my books would
Do it? Or my clothes?
Or friends? (O yes, don't worry
for you I'd be Judas).

But still you are there
In that great quiet immeasurable
Icy void with me running
After you. Wind whips my face
The ice lake cracks, the sound is terrible.
I cannot catch you up.
(Only thing is, I know how
To break the nightmare and be warm).

Please, please, may I take you out of cold?
I am waiting now, not pursuing.
But, can you tell me where you are?
You're frail but did you know
I can be strong, watching and writing?

3 xii 84

INDEX OF FIRST LINES

•